VAN GOGH'S
GHOST PAINTINGS

VAN GOGH'S
Ghost Paintings

Art and Spirit in Gethsemane

CLIFF EDWARDS

CASCADE *Books* · Eugene, Oregon

VAN GOGH'S GHOST PAINTINGS
Art and Spirit in Gethsemane

Copyright © 2015 Cliff Edwards. All rights reserved. Except for brief quotations in critical publications or reviews, no part of this book may be reproduced in any manner without prior written permission from the publisher. Write: Permissions, Wipf and Stock Publishers, 199 W. 8th Ave., Suite 3, Eugene, OR 97401.

Cascade Books
An Imprint of Wipf and Stock Publishers
199 W. 8th Ave., Suite 3
Eugene, OR 97401

www.wipfandstock.com

ISBN 13: 978-1-4982-0307-4

Cataloging-in-Publication data:

Edwards, Cliff, 1932–

Van Gogh's ghost paintings : art and spirit in Gethsemane / Cliff Edwards.

xii + 122 p. ; 23 cm. —Includes bibliographical references and index(es).

ISBN 13: 978-1-4982-0307-4

1. Gogh, Vincent van, 1853–1890—Religion. 2. Gogh, Vincent van, 1853–1890—Criticism and interpretation. I. Title.

ND653 G7 E337 2015

Manufactured in the U.S.A.

Scripture quotations are *from The Old and the New Testaments of the Holy Bible: Revised Standard Version*. Nashville, Thomas Nelson, 1971.

Quotations from Vincent van Gogh's letters appear by permission from *Vincent Van Gogh: The Letters: The Complete Illustrated and Annotated Edition*. Edited by Leon Jansen, Hans Luitjen and Nienke Bakker. Six Volumes. London: Thames and Hudson, in association with the Van Gogh Museum and the Huygens Institute, 2009.

Permission to reproduce photographs of letters and art works was procured from Vincent van Gogh Foundation/National Museum Vincent van Gogh, Amsterdam, and The Anderson Gallery, School of the Arts, Virginia Commonwealth University. Henry Hibbs Collection, 74.14.5

Dedication

I am delighted to dedicate this book to my father-in-law, Professor Fernand Lucien Marty, Professor Emeritus of French at the University of Illinois, whose passion for French literature and linguistics at several colleges and universities has inspired friends, family, and students for many decades. His early work on language learning labs in the 1940s and 50s, computer-assisted language learning in the 1960s and 70s and automatic text-to-speech systems in the 1980s and 90s broke boundaries and established new benchmarks for excellence across numerous disciplines. In all this work, Professor Marty created a long list of books, monographs, and articles that continue to guide and enrich others. More recently, Professor Marty returned his attention to French literature, with a particular focus on the writings of Emile Zola, including an expert critique of Vincent van Gogh's reading and comments on several of Zola's works. Our conversations on French culture and the arts go back many years. Almost thirty years ago Professor Marty helped me get access to French periodical sources important to my earliest book on Van Gogh, and he has since then kept me up on his research that bears on the life and work of Vincent Van Gogh in their cultural context. To Professor Marty's long list of books, monographs, and articles on the teaching of French and pioneer work with computers, he has now added a Van Gogh connection that has enriched many, and certainly stimulated me. Few scholars have continued active research and publishing into their tenth decade of life, and fewer still whose work continues to inform new understandings of the world around us. Professor Marty is one of those rare individuals. It is my personal honor to know him as his friend, colleague, and son-in-law. His continuing intellectual curiosity, his work ethic, and his practical wisdom all continue to inspire me, as they have so many others.

Table of Contents

List of Illustrations

Illustrations one through nine are printed with the permission of the Vincent van Gogh Foundation and the Van Gogh Museum in Amsterdam. Items ten and eleven are printed with the permission of the Anderson Gallery, Virginia Commonwealth University, Richmond, Virginia.

Foreword

To write a book on two paintings we have never seen is an accomplishment. For Cliff Edwards, the absence of the paintings is a kind of presence—revelatory at that. With *Van Gogh's Ghost Paintings*, which can be read as mystery narrative and detective adventure, Edwards adds a fourth work to his previous three on the artist: a Vincent van Gogh quartet. Here again we meet Vincent van Gogh as an artist in paint who is also a painter in words: "Let us work with our heart and love what we love." Vincent did. So does Cliff Edwards. Edwards suggests that Vincent "is doing in paint what Christ himself was doing in words. Vincent was painting parables." Consider this: "we shouldn't judge the Good Lord by this world, because it's one of his studies that turned out badly." On "a simple journey by train," which he compares to the journey of life, Vincent writes, "you go fast, but you can't distinguish any object very close up, and above all, you can't see the locomotive" (Letter 656). If we cannot see the locomotive pulling the artist's train, we can certainly feel that it is there and that this is a train worth riding. The text is punctuated and animated by questions, questions inviting us to climb aboard this train and join Edwards in his adventure and engagement with the life and death of Vincent van Gogh. Personal and geographical passages are welcoming as Edwards takes us with him to a monastery in Kyoto, Japan, where the quest begins. The Japanese and Zen connections are important: a concern of the text is "the recognition that there are symbols that reach across all cultural divides." We travel to Amsterdam, Otterlo, Paris, Arles, Montmajour, Auver-sur-Oise. Edwards's love and dedication show. He writes of "the antitheses that pulled Vincent's religious consciousness and artistic adventure taut." So we may be pulled taut in an appreciation of the emptiness and of the beauty of Vincent's

Gethsemane, of how the "erasure" of Gethsemane is the actualization of Gethsemane. We arrive at insight into the relation of religion and art—of how "religious art is a way of seeing rather than a what is seen . . . "

David Cain
Distinguished Professor Emeritus of Religion
University of Mary Washington

Acknowledgments

This book makes full use of the six volumes of *Vincent Van Gogh: The Letters* edited by Leon Jansen, Hans Luitjen, and Nienke Bakker, and published by Thames and Hudson in association with the Van Gogh Museum and the Huygens Institute in 2009. I have purposely used the new numbering system for Van Gogh's correspondence introduced by this new resource. I have also taken all quotations from Van Gogh's correspondence from this same source. Periods and spaces, capitalization and bold type in the English text are the translators' attempts to indicate features of Van Gogh's own handwriting in the original letters. Only ellipses composed of three periods with one space before and after each are my own addition to the quotations, indicating omissions I have made for purposes of focus and space.

I have used this new six volume resource and its electronic version on purpose so that every reader can explore the letters and related art. The source is also available on the internet by simply typing Ar in a web browser. One can then click on any piece of Van Gogh correspondence available and see it in English, the original Dutch, or French, or view a facsimile of the handwritten letter itself. If one clicks on "art work," one can view every art work available that is mentioned in each letter, in color when available. Clicking on "notes" gives one observations by the experts. I am deeply grateful for this new work, and believe it will add an important dimension to my book and will open doors to your own exploration of Van Gogh's life and art. An index at the end of my book will allow you to find and view many key works of art mentioned by Van Gogh and in my own discussions.

My personal gratitude to those who have provided the space and help for my research is so extensive that I must be satisfied with just a few brief references. Family and friends have provided the rich community in which I live and do my work, and deserve my deepest thanks. Colleagues at Virginia Commonwealth University in the religious studies program, the School of World Studies, The College of Humanities and Sciences, and the Anderson Gallery have given major inspiration and support. The staff of the Cabell Library has been a great help, and its staff in the Special Collections and Archives unit has given me a wonderful space for working with the Van Gogh volumes, as well as creative support and advice. Albertien Lykles-Livius in the Rights and Reproductions department of the Van Gogh Museum has been a wonderful help in arranging for the use of most of the images in this book. My current Commonwealth Society Class sponsored by the VCU School of the Arts has been a great inspiration. A special thanks is due, as in all my Van Gogh books, to Marcia Powell. Over thirty years ago Mrs. Powell, a teacher of French language and culture residing in Richmond, Virginia, translated every line of every letter of Van Gogh as a resource for our discussions of Van Gogh's paintings. That translation and those discussions have played a key role in my understanding of Van Gogh. Marcia Powell later gathered support to establish the Powell-Edwards Fund in Religion and the Arts at Virginia Commonwealth University, bringing major lecturers on the arts and conferences on religion and the arts to our campus. I am deeply grateful for her interest and labor. Chelsea Wilkinson, in the midst of preparing for graduate work in art therapy, has taken time to coach me in computer skills needed to get this text in order, and of course my editor, Dr. Chris Spinks, and the entire enterprise at Cascade Books have worked with me thoughtfully and with great expertise. I hope that it is clear to the reader that my gratitude to a great "cloud of witnesses" has shaped this book from beginning to end. What is best in it is to their credit, but I claim any and all its faults.

I

Locating the Ghost Paintings

Imagine that one of the most significant and revealing paintings by the world-famous artist Vincent van Gogh was never seen by anyone but the artist himself. Imagine that it was so important to the artist that he painted it twice, but he was so conflicted about it that he destroyed it twice. Those imaginings are reality. I call those paintings Van Gogh's "ghost paintings."

Vincent, as the artist preferred to be called, composed those two paintings during his most creative year as an artist. It was 1888, the same year he painted his *Sunflowers*, *The Yellow House*, *The Bedroom*, numerous blossoming orchards and fields of wheat, flower gardens and harvest scenes, fishing boats on the Mediterranean, and portraits of peasants, housewives, a postal worker, and children.

What is especially puzzling about Vincent creating and destroying his ghost paintings is that never before had he ever composed such a painting, and never again would he attempt such a painting. Those two destroyed paintings were unique among all his works. The closest he would come to those paintings was a copy of a work by Delacroix, but that was a copy, and that was not the subject he would choose for his own work.

I believe the two unique paintings Vincent created and destroyed are at least as important to understanding the artist and his work as are the two thousand or more paintings and drawings that do exist. I believe devoting attention to the ghost paintings will reveal an illuminating new dimension of Vincent's struggle to discover the spiritual dimension of art for the culture of his day and ours. I believe that hidden in those paintings and their story is Vincent's final word on "the art of life."

For me, the ghost paintings are much like Edgar Allan Poe's "Purloined Letter," hidden in such plain sight that their very existence, brief though it might have been, has remained largely invisible to us. My guess is that you have never heard of them, and I know you have never seen them. Yet I am convinced those two works did much to determine the course of Vincent's art for the last two years of his brief life as artist. In those two paintings he struggled with the meaning and direction of his intended contribution as an artist. The struggle and provisional solution arrived at by Vincent as revealed in those two works and their destruction played a critical role in the future direction of art, and contributed to the future relationship of religion and spirituality to the arts.

Let us go to the hiding place of those paintings and allow the artist himself to tell us their secret. On Sunday, July 8 or Monday, July 9 of 1888, worn out by a day of painting outside the city of Arles in Provence, just thirty miles from the Mediterranean, Vincent likely sat at a table in the Café de la Gare, on the ground floor of the Ginoux Inn. He often ate, drank, and wrote letters to his brother Theo at one of the café tables. One can see the very setting in the painting he titled *Café de la Nuit* (*The Night Café*). Upstairs was his rented room, filled with paintings drying before he could roll them up and send them to his brother Theo. Vincent was writing a six-page letter to Theo, manager of an art gallery on Montmartre in Paris. Most of the six pages dealt with responses to a now lost letter by Theo inquiring about debts Vincent may have left behind when he departed their apartment on February 19 for the sixteen-hour train trip to the south of France. Vincent informed Theo that he owed nothing to the paint-dealer Père Tanguy, but did owe Bing's Art Nouveau Shop for Japanese prints he had taken on consignment. Then, after commenting on newly completed drawings and a collection of recent paintings that were drying, Vincent began on page three of the letter some nine lines that are likely to surprise anyone who has studied the 1,500 or more drawings and paintings Vincent had completed from his beginning as an artist in 1880 to the moment he wrote that letter in the summer of 1888. He describes this painting whose subject matter stands alone among all his works. In a deceptively off-hand manner, he writes:

> I've scraped off one of the large painted studies. A *Garden of Ol-ives*—with a blue and orange Christ figure, a yellow angel—a piece of red earth, green and blue hills. Olive trees with purple and crim-son trunks, with grey green and blue foliage. Sky lemon yellow.
>
> I scraped it off because I tell myself it's wrong to do figures of that importance without a model. (Letter 637)

Vincent then abruptly turns to other subjects: the likelihood of Gauguin joining him at the Yellow House in Arles, news of other artists, Bing's col-lection of Japanese prints, and Pierre Loti's novel about Japan, *Madame Chrysanthemum*.

Vincent confesses he had destroyed his large painting of Jesus and an angel in the Garden of Olives, or Gethsemane. But his confession has its peculiarities. He had been worried that the expense for tubes of paint was driving his brother, who paid for them, to illness. He suggested to Theo that perhaps it would be best to give up painting in favor of the far less expensive pursuit of drawing (Letters 601, 615). Yet he admits here to the purposive loss of a good deal of paint. Even his use of the words "I tell myself" in "I tell myself it's wrong to do figures of that importance without a model" gives the impression that he is involved in a conflict within himself regarding his painting the figures of Christ and an angel. Perhaps he is hiding more than he is revealing regarding the significance of this painting and his decision to destroy it.

Nevertheless, we might treat the destruction of this one painting of a single scene selected from the life of Christ as an impulsive singularity among all his works if it were not for the fact that another surprise awaits us. Seventy-five days later, after some thirty-three more letters to Theo, Vincent has a second confession to make. On September 21, 1888, Vincent was in the midst of "a passion to make—an artist's house," planning his sun-flower decorations for the Yellow House, just a block from the café where he rooms and where he writes his letters to Theo. He is ecstatic that he will finally have a studio-home that will bring him "great peace of mind." In the midst of his euphoria, he makes his second confession:

> For the second time I've scraped off a study of a Christ with the an-gel in the Garden of Olives. Because here I see real olive trees. But I can't, or rather, I don't wish, to paint it without models. But I have it in my mind with color—the starry night, the figure of Christ blue, the strongest blues, and the angel broken lemon yellow. And all the purples from blood red purple to ash in the landscape. (Let-ter 685)

About two weeks later, on October 5, both the Garden of Olives or Gethsemane paintings were still on his mind when he wrote his young artist friend, Emile Bernard:

> I mercilessly destroyed an important canvas—a Christ with the angel in Gethsemane—as well as another one depicting the poet with a starry sky—because the form hadn't been studied from the model beforehand, necessary in such cases—despite the fact that the color was right. (Letter 698)

It appears that for over three months the Gethsemane painting with Christ and an angel had haunted Vincent. The first version with its yellow sky had over time transformed to a "starry night" scene. He admits that his Gethsemane painting was an "important canvas" and that "the color was right." The impulse to paint it remained too strong to resist, yet the conflicting feelings about having such a painting among his works necessitated the destruction of the second painting following in the wake of the destruction of the first. He has, of course, told us that he doesn't "wish to paint it without models," but why then attempt it twice? Further, what might he have imagined his models for such a painting would be? Would he have accepted someone who matched his imagined image of Christ or an angel? Or had he perhaps expected a vision of the scene to come to him in his act of painting? Further, Vincent tells us that his seeing "real olive trees" encouraged him to do the paintings. He would, in fact, draw and paint eighteen works focused on olive trees during his months in the asylum. Are those "olive trees" further attempts at the Mount of Olives Gethsemane scene? Might the very absence of Christ and an angel add to our sense of Vincent's struggle with the meaning of Gethsemane for himself as artist? Is there a movement toward a "negative way" to call the sacred to mind, a presence of Christ and angel as absent, refused, or erased essential to the depth of Vincent's search for a spirituality for the art of the future? Should showing a place in nature reflecting the Gethsemane scene bring the narrative to our memory? Or has Vincent refused the story as a visual narrative in favor of the here and now of actual olive orchards?

Exactly what is it about painting Jesus and the angel in Gethsemane that led to this double creation and double destruction during the height of the artist's creativity? Why had he never composed a scene from the life of Christ before, and why would he never compose such a scene again? These are all questions for which we will seek answers, or at least direction. I believe our very asking of these questions will take us more deeply than ever into the imagination and intentions of one of the greatest Western artists, and so into art as "spiritual biography" and an illumination of human creativity and the quest for meaning.

2

A Zen Master's Question

Before attempting answers to the several questions I've raised regarding the ghost paintings, allow me to introduce a quite different sort of question, one that is often addressed to me. I lecture on Vincent's art, life, and spiritual quest in museums, university classrooms, and religious institutions, in this country and abroad. During a question and answer period, I can count on one of the first questions asked to be some variation on the following: "What led you to get so interested in the painter Van Gogh?" Such a question might be expected, especially from those who know that my early studies and much of my teaching and writing have focused on the religious classics of the world's religions, especially on the relationship between Asian religious texts and practices and Western religious texts and practices. I believe my answer to that often-asked question may help you locate me and the direction my passion for the life and work of Vincent van Gogh has taken.

My early studies and degrees were in biblical studies and the history and literature of the world's religions, largely at Northwestern University, the University of Strasbourg in France, the University of Neuchatel in Switzerland, and Hebrew Union School of Bible and Archaeology in Jerusalem. But my growing interest in comparing Asian religions with Western traditions led me to travel to Japan, where I became interested in Buddhist religious art. That is when I was introduced to a zen master who was custodian of one of the world's most famous zen paintings.

It was the question posed by that zen master over a bowl of tea that initiated the journey of discovery that led to my passion for Vincent van Gogh's life and work and that has brought me to the book you have in hand. In 1971, fresh out of my Western studies, I traveled to Japan on a grant and was studying the Japanese language in a Kyoto language school. My teacher asked if I would be interested in teaching English to a zen monk. The monk was from a famous zen monastery in the city, Daitokuji, and was being sent to America to found a zen temple. I knew that a famous abbot at Daitokuji not only knew a great deal about the zen arts, but had in his temple treasury one of the most famous of all zen ink-paintings, Mu-ch'i's *Six Persimmons*. I traded English lessons for an introduction to my student's abbot, Kobori-Sohaku. The day came when I was ushered into his private chamber. Sitting on tatami mats, he served tea, and asked how he might help me. When I asked permission to see the famous zen ink painting, he smiled, and said, "If you can answer my question, I might be able to open our treasury and let you view the painting. My question is, why do the Japanese want to see Van Gogh's *Sunflowers* and you want to see Mu-ch'i's *Persimmons*? I will make it a simple koan. A Van Gogh sunflower and a Mu-ch'i persimmon: are they the same or different?" Perhaps there was some immediate response in koan style that might have suited the moment. But my thoughts were on how little I knew about either Van Gogh or the Japanese people's views on art. I promised Abbot Kobori I would attempt someday to solve his koan. That was the start of my life-long study of Van Gogh.

Beginning as an attempt to understand the relationship between Vincent's art and Japanese art, my interest broadened into a study of Vincent's spiritual quest and his way of seeing the world and living his life. After a stay at Daitokuji, I traveled to Amsterdam and Otterlo in Holland to see the greatest collections of Van Gogh's art, and to view some of his original letters to brother Theo. While in Amsterdam I bought my first set of volumes containing the letters of Van Gogh. Studying his letters fascinated me, for much of my early education had focused on interpreting the New Testament, and the New Testament is composed largely of letters. From Holland I traveled to Paris, and was fortunate enough to arrive during a major exhibition of Impressionist art at a museum on the Place de la Concorde. A banner over the exhibit contained a Van Gogh quotation: "We love Japanese art. All the Impressionists have that in common." A poster for the exhibit contained a copy Vincent had made of a woodblock print by the famous Japanese artist Hiroshige, along with this quotation: "All my work is based on Japanese art."

It was not until 1989 that I published my first book on Van Gogh. It was titled *Van Gogh and God*, and its fifth chapter titled "The Oriental Connection" was my first attempt to answer the koan posed by Abbot Kobori years before. But my attempt at an overview of Vincent's life and work in that book left me with many more questions than I had answered. I took a humbler approach in my second book, *The Shoes of Van Gogh* (2004). It responded to just nine of Vincent's paintings that I believed were most critical to understanding his life and art. Even that book seemed too broad, lacking the depth of focus necessary to get at the artist. My third book, *Mystery of the Night Café*, chose just a single painting, Vincent's *le Café de la Nuit*, and I felt that it got more deeply into the mind and vision of the artist than I had accomplished before.

Nevertheless, there remained a sense that something of vital importance had eluded me in all three of those books. Was there a natural progression from the whole of Van Gogh's life to a work on nine paintings to a work on a single painting? If so, where could one go beyond the focus on a single critical painting?

This year I decided to retrace my steps and begin again. Now I had an exciting new resource prepared by the Van Gogh Museum and the Huygens Institute in the Netherlands: *Vincent van Gogh—the Letters*, a six-volume set of all the existing letters sent and received by Vincent van Gogh, along with every remaining image he sketched, drew, and painted, plus every available image by other artists that he mentioned in his letters. Further, the scholars who created the six volumes also placed the material on the web (vangoghletters.org) and this electronic resource allowed me to study the facsimiles of all the letters as well. Years ago a Dutch scholar in Amsterdam had told me to take seriously the fact that Van Gogh "drew or painted" his letters, and one needed to study images of the actual letters to get the full sense of their meaning. This is now possible, and those images could be brought directly to my desk.

And so I began again and worked my way carefully through the six volumes and the facsimiles. It was during this past year of research that I made the discovery that I had missed in four decades of study and viewing. The discovery was the "ghost paintings," and the result of the discovery is this book. It is as though the next step on my journey of discovery had been waiting for me to listen to Vincent's words and see with new eyes what the artist himself was saying and seeing. It opened for me a new doorway to the artist's creative life and thought.

I invite you to join me in searching out the meaning of the ghost paintings, critical works that at the outset may seem inaccessible. Yet I believe the struggle necessary to discover what we can of these works will open a dimension of the artist's own spiritual search that has been locked away for too long. What we can know of them has eluded most, and generally been largely ignored even when noticed. As far as I can find, they have never been assessed as having the critical role they deserve. But to locate these paintings and their significance, we must be willing to open our vision to that of the artist himself, to appreciate the power of negation, the odd twists and turns of the play of presence and absence, the revealing nature of irony, paradox, contradiction, and destruction that lurk in some of the deeper recesses of symbolic expression. We must be willing to examine the consequences of life's critical choices, the meaning of roads not taken as well as those traveled. In a sense, this search for the significance of Vincent's ghost paintings promises to bring me full circle back to themes met in Asian art and spiritual philosophy, and so back to the question posed by Abbot Kobori at that zen monastery in Japan. The ghost paintings, I think we will find, are in some ways like a koan waiting to be solved. They will confront us with frustrations, puzzles, surprises, and perhaps finally will offer some enlightenment to the dedicated seeker.

As I sit viewing my computer screen, I look above it to the wall where I have taped four quotations that remind me of the wider significance of this search for the ghost paintings, as well as provide a clue or two that have helped me along the way. Perhaps these quotations may be of help to you as well on our search for the meaning of the ghost paintings.

The first quotation I have taken from a famous philosopher-theologian who escaped Nazi Germany many years ago to teach in the United States. Several times, while I was a student at Northwestern University, I took the elevated train to the University of Chicago to hear him deliver lectures. These words from his little book, *Dynamics of Faith*, constantly remind me of the illumination that can come through the arts: "All arts create symbols for a level of reality that cannot be reached in any other way. . . . In the Creative work of art we encounter reality in a dimension which is closed for us without such works."[1] Tillich goes on to claim that such art "also unlocks dimensions and elements of the soul which correspond to the dimensions

1. Tillich, *Dynamics of Faith*, 42.

and elements of reality." If Tillich was right, imagine how impoverished our lives would be without the experience of creative works of art. We would be robbed of a depth dimension of our world, and there would be rooms in our own souls locked away from us. And so the question asked by Abbot Kobori becomes a question of the depth dimension of cultures East and West, the recognition that there are symbols that reach across all cultural divides, from sunflowers to persimmons, and so issue a global invitation to discover ways to live more completely, more creatively.

The second quotation above my desk is from a masterpiece of literature by Marcel Proust, a work of many hundreds of pages that is more often talked about than read. The work is titled *A la recherche du temps perdu*, sometimes translated *Remembrance of Things Past*. The words of Proust that tell me something about the very reason I view and study the life and work of Vincent van Gogh with such interest and persistence are: "The only true journey, the only bath in the Fountain of Youth, would be not to visit new lands but to possess other eyes, to see the universe through the eyes of another."[2] If life's true journey is to share in the vision of others, why not choose the most creative eyes one can find? For me, this has led to the attempt to share the vision of Vincent van Gogh's extraordinary creative eyes. Those eyes have illuminated the life presence of sunflowers and wheatfields, cypresses and blossoming orchards. They have seen and shared with sensitivity and compassion the faces of peasants and miners, weavers and housewives, children and prostitutes. They are the eyes of an artist who searched his own face in times of discovery and failure, loneliness, and illness. Perhaps our sharing in his vision will offer a personal transformation akin to Proust's promised "bath in the Fountain of Youth."

The third quotation is by George Steiner, a fascinating critic of culture who has written twenty-six books over half a century, including a book titled *My Unwritten Books*, from which I take these words:

> A book unwritten is more than a void. It accompanies the work one has done like an active shadow, both ironic and sorrowful. It is one of the lives we could have lived, one of the journeys we did not take. Philosophy teaches that negation can be determinant. It is more than a denial of possibility. Privation has consequences we cannot foresee or gauge accurately. It is the unwritten book which might have made the difference. Which might have allowed one to fail better. Or perhaps not.[3]

2. Proust, *Remembrance of Things Past*, 3:762
3. Steiner, *My Unwritten Books*, ix.

Those words written by Steiner at the University of Cambridge in 2006 describe much of what I have been seeking in the two ghost paintings of Van Gogh. Those paintings go beyond the "book unwritten" to a work twice created and twice destroyed. That they followed the rest of Vincent's work like an "active shadow," and that they involved a "journey" he took only provisionally, a journey that he then wrapped in a "negation" that made "the difference," seems evident to me, though solving the meaning of that negation and difference requires a steep climb.

The fourth and final slip of paper taped above my computer screen is by Vincent van Gogh himself, and has served me as a clue and goad toward solving the meaning of the ghost paintings. Vincent had written a letter to brother Theo around September 5 of 1883. Soaked from painting "crooked, windswept trees" in a rain-storm, Vincent mused on the way sorrow developed a sense of character in human beings. He concluded: "Yes, for me the drama of a storm in nature, the drama of sorrow in life, is the best. A 'paradou' is beautiful, but Gethsemane is more beautiful still" (Letter 381). Vincent was likely thinking of the enclosed garden named "paradou" in an Emile Zola novel he had recently read, *The Sin of Abbé Mouret* (who, interestingly, has his ear cut off at the end of the novel). That garden for both Zola and Vincent is the reflection of the Bible's Garden of Paradise. Vincent's preference for one garden over the other, Gethsemane over Paradise, may well be a clue to the puzzle of the artist's choice of the one biblical scene he selected for painting twice, and perhaps also a clue to their destruction.

Our search for the deeper significance of Vincent's ghost paintings and their vision of Gethsemane requires at least a thumbnail sketch of his life that led from a Dutch parsonage to his journey to Arles. And so I provide a sketch of his life in the next chapter, followed by a chapter on his decision to journey to Arles where he would create and would destroy the Gethsemane paintings.

3

Quest for the Artist

Vincent van Gogh arrived in southern France at the old Roman city of Arles on February 20, 1888. He was not yet thirty-five years old, and had been painting for less than eight years. After two years living with his younger brother Theo in a Paris apartment, Vincent had become disgusted with the constant bickering among warring factions of the city's artists. He was ill from drinking "too much bad wine," and was suffering from the freezing weather of a very severe Paris winter. He decided he must regain his health and paint in the light such favorite artists as Delacroix and Monticelli had enjoyed in the warmth and clarity of the Mediterranean sun. He took the train along the "route of the sun" from Paris some 482 miles south to Arles in Provence, a trip of about sixteen hours. In a later letter to Theo, Vincent emphasized the artistic reasons for the move:

> My dear brother, you know that I came to the south and threw myself into my work for a thousand reasons. To want to see another light, to believe that looking at nature under a brighter sky can give us a more accurate idea of the Japanese way of feeling and drawing. Wanting, finally, to see this stronger sun, because one feels that without knowing it one couldn't understand the paintings of Delacroix from the point of view of execution, technique, and because one feels that the colours of the prism are veiled in mist in the north. (Letter 801)

His assertion "I threw myself into my work" is an understatement. He would remain in Arles for 444 days, during which he would create two hundred paintings and over a hundred drawings and watercolors. As the art specialist Ronald Pickvance wrote in *Van Gogh in Arles*, that accomplishment remains "a prodigal and quite astonishing outpouring, sustaining a pace that no other artist of the nineteenth century could match."[1]

Van Gogh was surprised to find that Arles was under a thick layer of snow when he arrived, but even that did not stop him from painting almost from the very day of his arrival. As the snow melted and spring arrived, he discovered that Arles had periods with a powerful "mistral" wind that made painting difficult, but he adjusted as best he could to the difficulties. Further, he found that there really was no established colony of artists with whom he could associate and exchange ideas. Fortunately for us, this gave him even more reason to write letters to Theo and to a series of artist friends, including Gauguin and Bernard. In those letters, he describes the landscape, inhabitants of Arles, his paintings and drawings, and the questions he was struggling with regarding his mission as artist. But there remained the issue of loneliness and isolation. He found that in that city of twenty-three thousand, he was the only Dutchman, and though his French was good, the people of Arles spoke a dialect of Provence that made communication difficult. He also found that most of the people of Arles looked upon foreign painters as either wealthy dandies playing at art or as madmen. A plan to bring other artists to Arles to form a "monastery" of artist-monks sharing meals and painting together grew in his mind and in his letters to Theo. It would lead to an invitation to Paul Gauguin to come to Arles as the "abbot" for such a community. Gauguin did eventually come to Arles, but for only two months, and then Vincent van Gogh was alone again, alone and hospitalized.

We will have a number of occasions in the pages ahead to look back at Vincent's life and art before his arrival in Arles, but we must remind ourselves at this point that even at age thirty-five, Vincent had already been through much, suffered several life-changing failures, and labored hard to find his own direction and mission in life. He carried a good deal of baggage with him to Arles, had much to sort out, and had critical decisions to make about his intent as an artist. Even a few pages sketching the journey he had already undergone may be a help as we seek to locate the place and critical role of his ghost paintings.

1. Pickvance, *Van Gogh in Arles*, 11.

Who was this strange Dutchman who arrived at the Arles railroad station on February 20, 1888? Biographies of the artist are easily located, psychological studies of the artist are readily found, and colorful picture books of his art are offered on discount shelves of almost every large bookstore. Similarly, several one-volume abridged collections of his letters are available, selected by museum directors, artists, and poets. Sites on the internet take us to Vincent's paintings, drawings, and letters. Above all there is the amazing new six-volume set I mentioned earlier, *Vincent Van Gogh: The Letters,* and its website is prepared by the experts at the Van Gogh Museum in Amsterdam and the Huygens Institute in The Hague.

I will offer here simply a thumb-nail sketch of Vincent's life before his arrival in Arles. Such a sketch should at least hint at the fact that Vincent had already lived a surprisingly varied and often difficult life. He had been raised in a parsonage in a small village surrounded by fields, forests, and the homes of peasants. He eventually worked in three world capitals known for their art and culture. He was required to employ three different languages for daily communication at various times in his life. He had served the rich and lived among the poor. He had suffered serious deprivations, some due to unavoidable circumstances and others due to his voluntary ascetic practices. Vincent, even at age thirty-five, had developed a complex character formed in part by the immense variety of the influences of his time and place, his family, his aspirations, his suffering and failures, and his passionate reading of scores of books and equally passionate viewing of hundreds if not thousands of paintings, drawing, and prints. We will provide a few way-markers that suggest the route his "pilgrimage" took. Citing a few passages from his letters may also help us locate his feelings and voice.

Vincent was born on March 30, 1853, a year after Pastor Theodorus and Anna van Gogh's first child was stillborn. Following Vincent's birth were the births of five siblings, Anna, Theodorus, Elizabeth, Wilhelmina, and Cornelis. The Dutch Reformed parsonage where Vincent spent most of his first fifteen years, about 40 percent of his lifetime, was in the agricultural village of Zundert. The village, near the Belgian border, was largely Roman Catholic, hence Pastor Van Gogh's small congregation had only about a hundred and twenty Dutch Reformed parishioners. Apart from two years at a boarding school in nearby Zevenbergen and two years at a secondary school in Tilburg, Vincent's chief setting was the parsonage with its regimen of home-schooling, daily family prayers, Bible-readings, and weekly services and sermons in the small church beside the parsonage.

The deep impression these parsonage days within a setting of fields and peasant cottages had on Vincent, is illuminated by his comments later in life, after his father's death and during his own illness. He wrote Theo on January 22, 1889:

> During my illness I again saw each room in the house at Zundert, each path, each plant in the garden, the views round about, the fields, the neighbors, the cemetery, the church, our kitchen garden behind— right up to the magpies' nest in a tall acacia in the cemetery . . . to remember all this there's now only Mother and me. (Letter 741)

As his words illustrate, Vincent's sensitivity to place, feeling for details of nature, and keen visual memory all become an important part of his outlook as artist.

The two themes of church and art were a family heritage. Father and grandfather were clergy and three of Pastor Van Gogh's brothers were well-off art-dealers and collectors. At age sixteen, in the summer of 1869, it was likely the influence and connections of those three uncles that dictated Vincent's placement as a junior clerk in The Hague branch of Goupil and Company with its several art galleries and business in paintings and art-prints. Vincent's first preserved letters are from his fourth year with Goupil to his younger brother Theo. When Theo was placed in the Brussels branch of Goupil in 1873, a regular correspondence between the two brothers began. Chief subjects were family, paintings, prints, and books. In 1873 Vincent was transferred to London, and his serious religious interests emerged, intensified by daily Bible reading and prayer when he was transferred to Paris in 1875. Many of his letters to Theo during this period are a confusing patchwork of Bible quotations, prayers, and church hymns. The Goupil period comes to a surprising end in 1876 when Vincent is dismissed from his position. His leaving for Christmas vacation to be with his family without Goupil's blessing may have been one of the contributing causes. Though Vincent says little about the dismissal, it was likely a shattering experience of failure, though his later ponderings of the event may indicate that he had become gradually disillusioned with the management of Goupil. In a letter to Theo on December 11, 1882, Vincent compared the deterioration of art in a favorite illustrated magazine with the policies of Obach, the manager of Goupil's London branch:

> And now, everything is gone—once again the material in place of the moral. Do you know what I think of the folder I'm sending

you? It's just like the way of talking that, for example, Obach, the manager of G@C. in London, goes in for. And that is successful . . . It's just that it makes me sad, it takes away my pleasure, it upsets me, and I no longer know what I, for my part, should or should not do. (Letter 293)

Here we get some glimpse of Vincent's idealism regarding the arts, and the continuing pain connected to his dismissal and sense of failure regarding his days with Goupil and Company.

Reduced to answering advertisements for job openings, Vincent found a position teaching at a school for boys in England, and then work assisting a Methodist minister in the London area. Though little pay was involved, Vincent's sense of fulfillment in a church vocation is obvious. A letter to Theo on November 3, 1876, contains the full text of Vincent's first sermon and these words indicating his sense of mission:

When I stood in the pulpit I felt like someone emerging from a dark, underground vault into the friendly daylight. And it's a wonderful thought that from now on, wherever I go, I'll be preaching the Gospel- to do that *well* one must have the Gospel in his heart, may He bring this about. (Letter 96)

After reading Vincent's expression of his joy and fulfillment in preaching, it may seem strange that within two months he was back in Holland working as a bookseller's clerk. It is likely that a family council met and decided that it was not proper for a Van Gogh to work for little more than room and board as a Methodist pastor's assistant. One of the wealthy uncles arranged Vincent's new employment until arrangements could be made to have him tutored for entry exams to a proper theological school. This long and arduous preparation in Greek and Latin, history and mathematics, was discouraging to Vincent, and he soon transferred to a Belgian Missionary Training School that allowed him a probationary assignment as evangelist in a village in the Belgian mining district called the Borinage. Evidence indicates Vincent struggled to imitate the life of Christ, living among the mining families, descending into the mines, and nursing workers hurt in mine disasters. His manner of living and working in poverty with the laborers shocked both his family and the Missionary Board. His appointment ended in dismissal by the Board.

Refusing to return home from the mining district, Vincent wrote perhaps his most poignant letter, admitting his failures and deep discouragement to Theo. Written from the mining village of Cuesmes about June 24,

1880, he admitted he was now "an impossible and suspect character in the family," a "prisoner in penury, excluded from participating in this work or that." He described himself as a "bird at moulting time," or a "caged bird" in need of friendship and love that might "open the prison." He wrote that "my torment is none other than this, what could I be good for, couldn't I serve and be useful in some way." His deep discouragement included his experience with the church and his fellow evangelists: "There's an old, often detestable, academic school, the abomination of desolation. . . . Their God is like the God of Shakespeare's drunkard, Falstaff, 'The inside of a church'" (Letter 155).

Between that letter of June, 1880 and his next letter to Theo on August 20, a transformation took place. Vincent the failure, rejected for service to the church, was now "sketching large drawings after Millet." He declared to Theo, "If only I can go on working, I'll recover somehow" (Letter 156). The work he had decided upon was to prepare himself as an artist to draw and paint among laborers, miners, and peasants. By September 24, a letter to Theo described how he had learned "to see with a quite different eye" in his "ordeal of poverty," and that through picking up "my pencil" everything "has changed for me" (Letter 158).

Coming through these ordeals and failures determined to be an artist, Vincent was still far from the end of the pilgrimage leading to Arles and his ghost paintings. By 1881 he had returned to his parents' parsonage, now in the village of Etten, to save money while learning to draw peasants at work. His falling in love with his widowed cousin, Kee Vos, who had been vacationing at the parsonage with his parents, led to another major failure and serious rupture with family. Kee Vos, in continued mourning for her husband, answered Vincent's passionate declaration of love with a "No, Never, Never" (Letter 179). Vincent persisted against his family's advice, and by December an argument with Pastor Van Gogh led to Vincent being ordered out of the parsonage at Christmas.

Another period of poverty and failure awaited him in The Hague, where he moved to continue his art. With only the money sent him by brother Theo and occasional gifts from his father, Vincent not only struggled to afford art supplies, but also supported in his studio an ill prostitute who had a small daughter and was pregnant with the child of another client. When family found he was living with a prostitute, and in fact proposed marrying her, he was threatened with the loss of financial support, and even with the possibility of being committed to a mental institution as incompetent. But Vincent's taking the seriously ill woman, Clasina Maria Hoornik (Sien) to a clinic may well have saved her life and the life of her baby boy. He describes seeing the child in its cradle in terms of one of his favorite New Testament scenes:

> I can't look at the last piece of furniture without emotion, for it's a strong and powerful emotion that grips a person when one has sat beside the woman he loves with a child in the cradle near her. And even if it was a hospital where she lay and I sat with her, it's always the eternal poetry of Christmas night with the baby in the manger as the old Dutch painters conceived of it, and Millet and Breton—that light in the darkness—a brightness in the midst of a dark night. (Letter 245)

He later cited Jesus' words against his family's rejection of Sien: "and I for my part understand the words of Jesus, who said to the superficially civilized, the respectable people of His time, 'The harlots go BEFORE you'" (Letter 388). Vincent's loss of his one chance at a family, problematic as it was, seems to have haunted him for the rest of his life. The circumstances leading to Vincent's separation from Sien and her children is uncertain. It involved the realization of all involved that Vincent as artist could not support them, and their remaining together likely meant the loss of any support from the Van Gogh family. But it may also have involved Sien's decision, influenced perhaps by her mother and brother, to return to the streets. Whatever the whole story involved, Vincent's leaving for a desolate section of the Netherlands called Drenthe involved a deep sense of loss, guilt, and certainly suffering for all involved. From Drenthe, he wrote Theo that "the fate of the woman and the fate of my little boy and the other child cut my heart to shreds." He went on:

> rather than separating, I would have risked one more attempt by marrying her and going to live in the country. . . . But I believed one thing, that this was the right course, even despite the temporary financial drawbacks, and that not only could it have been her salvation but would also have put an end to great inner struggle for me, which has now, unhappily doubled for me. And I would rather have seen it through to the bitter end. (Letter 390)

Lonely and discouraged, Vincent soon left Drenthe to return to the family parsonage, now in the village of Nuenen in Holland. Though Pastor Van Gogh, his wife, and family seem to have tried hard to accommodate Vincent as struggling artist, he describes his feelings of rejection, attributing it to "a clergyman's vanity." He describes to Theo his belief that "Ma and Pa" think of him as a "large, shaggy dog": "Then—the dog might perhaps bite— if he were to go mad—and the village constable would have to come round and shoot him dead" (Letter 413). In spite of strained relations within the family, as well as a crisis involving a neighbor's daughter who apparently fell in love with Vincent and attempted suicide, the artist worked long and hard in the fields and homes of peasant farmers and weavers to improve his drawing and become a true peasant-artist like Millet.

On March 26, 1885, Pastor Van Gogh died of a heart attack upon reaching home after making pastoral calls. He was just sixty-three and appeared in good health, and so the sudden death was a shock to the family. Vincent memorialized his father's death with a painting of the pastor's Bible beside a snuffed out candle. That was a traditional enough *memento mori* theme, but Vincent added his own final word to disputes he had long had with his father, who rejected as immoral the new French literature Vincent favored. A bright yellow paperback book, Zola's new novel *La Joie de vivre* (*The Joy of Living*) is pushed up against his father's large open Bible. The subtlety of Vincent's painting, however, has eluded most viewers. The Bible is clearly depicted as open to the prophet Isaiah, chapter 53, the Suffering Servant Songs, and the novel *La Joie de vivre* only appears to be a stark contrast to the Bible. The actual story Zola tells in his novel is of a young orphan girl who is in fact a suffering servant whose life follows the pattern of the Isaiah passage. Zola, Vincent indicates, is a prophet for our time, and perhaps the role of prophet was intended to extend to Vincent's own aspirations in art as well.

Within a month of his father's death, Vincent was also completing what he hoped might be a masterwork, proving his maturing as an artist, the painting we call *The Potato-Eaters*. The crudeness of the scene, which led to much criticism, was explained by Vincent:

> You see, I really have wanted to make it so that people get the idea that these folk, who are eating their potatoes by the light of their little lamp, have tilled the earth themselves with these hands they are putting in the dish, and so it speaks of MANUAL LABOR, and—that they have thus honestly *earned* their food . . .

> And likewise, it would be wrong, to my mind, to give a peasant painting a certain conventional smoothness. If a peasant picture smells of bacon, smoke, potato steam—fine, that's not unhealthy— if a stable smells of manure—very well, that's what a stable's for—if

a field has an odour of ripe wheat or potatoes or—of guano and manure—that's really healthy—particularly for city folk. (Letter 497)

Within a year, Vincent's mother was required to leave the Nuenen parsonage to make room for a new pastor. She moved with her daughter Wilhelmina (Wil) to Breda and then Leyden. Mother Anna would outlive her son Vincent by sixteen years, and sister Wil would spend her last decades in an asylum.

Vincent left the parsonage, his studio in Nuenen, and Holland itself forever, arriving in the Belgian city of Antwerp on November 24, 1885. City life, the port's wharfs, the museums, and drawing and painting classes in Antwerp's Academy of Fine Arts stimulated Vincent. Japanese prints he found in the city were soon hanging on the walls of his rented room. But the money Theo sent was not enough to pay for painting and eating, and so Vincent often chose to go hungry, suffered illness, and lost many of his teeth. By the End of February, 1886, he took a night train to Paris, without consulting Theo. He sent a scrap of paper to Theo's gallery asking that he come get him at the Louvre and allow him to share Theo's small apartment.

From the end of February of 1886 until his leaving for Arles in Provence on February 19, 1888, the two brothers lived together. Vincent arranged displays of Japanese prints in Paris restaurants, painted in increasingly bright colors inside and outside the city with such artists as Camille Pissarro and Emile Bernard, and introduced Theo to many of the new painters, inspiring him to champion their cause in Goupil's Montmartre Gallery. Though Vincent's stubborn arguments sometimes weighed very heavily on the exhausted Theo, a letter from Theo to sister Wil soon after Vincent left for Arles reveals how close the brothers had become over those two years. The previously unpublished letter appears in Jan Hulsker's valuable study of the brothers, *Vincent and Theo Van Gogh: A Dual Biography*. We will allow an excerpt from that letter to sum up Theo's view of their years together in Paris:

> When he came here two years ago I had not expected that we would become so much attached to each other, for now that I am alone in the apartment there is a decided emptiness about me. If I can find someone I will take him in, but it is not easy to replace someone like Vincent. It is unbelievable how much he knows and what a sane view he has of the world. If he still has some years to live I am certain that he will make a name for himself. Through

him I got to know many painters who regarded him very highly. He is one of the avant-garde for new ideas, that is to say, there is nothing new under the sun so it would be better to say: for the regeneration of the old ideas which through routine have been diluted and worn out. In addition he has such a big heart that he always tries to do something for others. It's a pity for those who cannot understand him or refuse to do so.[2]

Hulkser's study of the brothers also provides us a picture of Vincent's gesture of gratitude toward Theo for the work they had shared and the prints they had collected during their two years together in Paris. Reflecting on his own coming loneliness, Vincent likely wished to soften the loneliness Theo might feel in his absence. Hulsker quotes a remembrance of the artist Emile Bernard:

> One evening Vincent said to me: "I am leaving tomorrow, let us arrange the studio together in such a way that my brother will think me still here." He nailed Japanese prints against the wall and put canvases on the easels, leaving others in a heap on the floor.[3]

Perhaps the fastidious Theo smiled at the rather chaotic scene Vincent left behind, reminded of their differences in temperament as well as of Vincent's "big heart."

2. Huskler, *Vincent and Theo Van Gogh,* 267–68.
3. Ibid., 260–61.

4

The Pilgrimage from Paris to Arles

Vincent's decision to leave the comfortable space Theo had provided for him in the Montmartre apartment in Paris was critical to the remainder of his life and the transformation of his art. He might have easily continued to live with his brother in the city that was the art center of the Western world. He would have enjoyed regular room and board, fellowship with some of the greatest artists of his era, cafés willing to show his paintings, and the inspiration of the treasures of Europe's greatest museums. His choice was to move almost five hundred miles from Theo and the resources of Paris to live as a suspect foreigner in rented rooms above laborers' saloons in a strange city. Locating each day's work in an unfamiliar countryside without the companionship of other artists was either a crazy or courageous personal choice. In a sense it was an act of destruction, an erasure of a certain degree of orderliness among friends, acquaintances, and familiar streets and a venturing out into chaos and the unknown. True, Vincent had problems he hoped to leave behind, the freezing winters of the north, his own heavy drinking and its physical toll, and the sectarian arguments of the Paris art-scene. It is also true that certain promises drew him south: the Mediterranean sun he found in the paintings of Delacroix and Monticelli, and the health he believed resided outside the confusion of cities in a life-giving countryside. But Vincent's move to Arles would be no easy journey in spite of the lifeline of Theo's continued support.

Vincent already knew what homeless wandering among strangers could mean. In 1882 he had written Theo of an incident in which his cousin, the established artist Anton Mauve, had mocked him for his peculiarities:

> if Mauve imitates and parrots me, saying, 'that's the face you pull,' this is how you talk, I'll reply, My dear fellow, if you had spent damp nights in the streets of London or cold nights in the Borinage as I have done—hungry, roofless, feverish, perhaps you'd also have the occasional ugly tic, and something in your voice, to show for it. (Letter 221)

Might similar hardships await him deep into the south, far from Paris and Theo? Vincent seems to have chosen the role of a homeless artist, knowing the risks and accepting suffering as essential to his mission. The ordeal was necessary for the development of an art that was to be free, exploratory, open to a new clarity of atmosphere and light. In a larger sense, Vincent seems to have viewed his choice as the only one consistent with his own sense of life as a call to pilgrimage.

The call to pilgrimage, solitude, sacrifice, and suffering came directly from Vincent's own interpretation of biblical stories as well as the new literature that applied scriptural truth to contemporary life. So the painting done soon after his father's death in 1885, with its clear citation of the "suffering servant song" of Isaiah chapter 53, stands as an emblem of his vision of life consistent with both the Bible and Zola's novel focused on the sufferings of an orphan girl, the novel Vincent placed beside that open Bible. Vincent's earlier sermon preached to a Methodist congregation in England in 1876 calls for that same pattern, bringing to mind key biblical texts, Bunyan's *Pilgrim's Progress*, art works, and poetry on the themes of the chosen homelessness of pilgrimage, and the expectation of suffering that is joined to hope and joy:

> We are pilgrims in the earth and strangers—we come from afar and we are going far.—The journey of our life goes from the loving breast of our Mother on earth to the arms of our Father in heaven. Everything on earth changes—we have no abiding city here—it is the experience of everybody: That it is God's will that we should part with what we dearest have on earth. (Sermon enclosed with Letter 96)

Vincent's sermon sounds much like his blueprint for the trajectory of his life, a predictor of his leaving Paris, which in spite of all its treasures was "no abiding city." He must part from Theo's apartment to become once more a pilgrim and stranger on earth in Provence. The sermon goes on to describe "a very beautiful painting" he once saw. His description focused on its hills and sunset and autumn leaves, with a pilgrim walking the road toward a high mountain. An "angel of God," who brings to Vincent's mind Paul's words "sorrowful yet always rejoicing," is asked by the pilgrim, "Does the road go uphill all the way?" The answer, taken from a Christina Rossetti's poem, is "Yes to the very end." It is as though there is no way Vincent could have remained in a comfortable Paris apartment and been true to his vision of life.

We might cite one more example of Vincent's image of life's pilgrimage, displaced, or transformed by him to a call to suffering on the way not to the heavenly city but to a new art capable of comforting contemporary humanity. Writing fellow Dutch artist Anton van Rappard in 1881, an artist Vincent believed to be too comfortable, traditional, and timid in his art, he challenged:

> I'm not ashamed of being a man, of having principles and faith. But where do I want to drive people, especially myself? To the open sea. And which doctrine do I preach? People, let us surrender our souls to our cause and let us work with our heart and love what we love. (Letter 188)

In that same letter to Rappard, Vincent warns of the difficulties a life on the "open sea" will bring:

> Someone who works regularly at the academy as you do must feel rather out of his element when, instead of knowing in advance, today I have to do this or that, he must daily *improvise* or rather *create* his working environment.

Vincent went on to explain to Rappard that leaving the academy behind would mean days when one felt "that the ground was giving way under your feet." That, of course, is exactly what Vincent sought in his pilgrimage to Arles, a voyage out on the open sea, the ground giving way under his feet, a "not knowing" that would require improvisation, or better, the need to "create" each day the quest for a new art for a new age.

In 1888, now in Arles, living and working close by the Arles railroad yard, tracks, and overpass, Vincent played a creative variation on his image describing life's journey with its vertiginous transformations and its continuing mystery. He improvised on his daily experience in the neighborhood of the railroad station. Beginning by musing on the death of one of their uncles, he wove together images of the face of the dead, a child's eyes, and a train trip:

> Which is why in the present case of our uncle's death, the dead man's face was tranquil, serene and grave. When it's a fact that, while living, he was scarcely like that, neither when young nor when old. So often I've noticed an effect like that when looking at a dead man as if to question him. And that's one proof for me—not the most weighty—of an existence beyond the grave.
>
> And a baby in its cradle, also, if you look at it at your ease, has the infinite in its eyes. In fact, I know nothing about it, but precisely this feeling of *not knowing* makes the real life that we're living at present comparable to a simple journey by train. You go fast, but you can't distinguish any object very close-up, and above all, you can't see the locomotive. (Letter 656)

5

Gethsemane in the Bible

We will soon return to Vincent in Arles and the mystery of the two paintings he created and destroyed there. But first we should view what was likely a chief resource for those paintings, the Gethsemane story as narrated in the gospels of the New Testament. Perhaps we will find clues there to the special attraction and deep meaning that scene had for the artist. There may be some answer to the question, "Why did Vincent select Gethsemane as the one moment in the life of Christ he wished to compose as a 'large' and 'important' painting, and why did he decide to destroy that work?"

It is in the Gospels of Matthew, Mark, and Luke that we find the Gethsemane story of Jesus' distress and prayer on or near the Mount of Olives while his disciples sleep. The scene leads into that of Jesus' betrayal, arrest, and trials leading to the crucifixion. As the story unfolds, after Jesus and his disciples have their last supper together, Jesus leads them to the Mount of Olives, and from there to Gethsemane, though Luke simply calls it "the place." The word "Gethsemane," which occurs only in Mark and Matthew, is simply composed of the Aramaic words meaning "oil press," no doubt indicating that the place was named for nearby stone presses for grinding the oil from olives harvested at the Mount of Olives. The Gospel of John lacks this larger story, telling only that Jesus "went forth with his disciples across the Kidron valley, where there was a garden" and it is there that Jesus is arrested (John 18:1–4). It is John alone who tells of a "garden" or "enclosure."

Likely the Gospel of Mark contains the earliest account, with Matthew and Luke borrowing heavily, though adding certain details unique to each. One of many rich resources for those interested in modern textual problems and the inter-relationships of the three accounts is to be found in the respected scholar Raymond Brown's two-volume study, *The Death of the Messiah: From Gethsemane to the Grave*. As his sub-title indicates, Gethsemane acts as the doorway to the Passion story of Christ, focused on the trials, crucifixion, and resurrection stories. Adela Yarbro Collins's volume on the Gospel of Mark in the Hermeneia series of Bible Commentaries also illuminates relevant aspects of the Gethsemane narrative, citing a wide variety of suggestive scholarly interpretations of the text.

We should pay special attention to the fact that painting the Gethsemane episode required Vincent to choose among many possible scenes from the life of Christ, a score of them far more popular than Jesus' agony in Gethsemane. As the religious studies scholar and art historian Diane Apostolos-Cappadona writes in her *Dictionary of Christian Art*: "The Agony in the Garden was rarely depicted in Christian art." She notes that the earliest example of the Gethsemane scene is on fourth-century sarcophagi, that the event was rarely illustrated in medieval literary dramas, but that it did receive "some artistic attention in the nineteenth-century revival of Christian art."[1] A volume focused on scenes popular in Reformation art, William Halewood's *Six Subjects of Reformation Art: A Preface to Rembrandt*, notes the popularity of such scenes as Jesus' calling Matthew, the Raising of Lazarus, the Prodigal Son, the preaching of John the Baptist and Jesus, Jesus blessing the children and healing the sick, the conversion of Paul, and the crucifixion scene. Gethsemane is absent from the popular choices of Reformation art, as it was also largely absent from early Christian art and Catholic art. It may well be that Gethsemane's picture of a vulnerable and uncertain Christ who wished to avoid the "cup of suffering" made both theologians and artists uneasy. Perhaps that is also the reason for the absence of the Gethsemane scene from the tradition of the Stations of the Cross.

For many centuries artists have tended to focus on such scenes as the annunciation to Mary, the nativity scene, Mary holding the Christ-child, the flight to Egypt by the Holy Family, the temptation story, the call of the disciples, scenes of Jesus teaching and healing, Jesus with three disciples on the Mount of Transfiguration, the Palm Sunday entry to Jerusalem,

---

1. Apostolos-Cappadona, *Dictionary of Christian Art*, 20–21.

cleansing of the Temple, arrest, trials, and crucifixion of Jesus, removal from the cross, entombment, resurrection, and risen Jesus with disciples at Emmaus. John's Gospel contributed a unique collection of popular scenes of its own, including Jesus with the woman at the well, the raising of Lazarus, and the risen Christ's appearance to Mary Magdalene and to Thomas. Neil MacGregor's *Seeing Salvation: Images of Christ in Art* might provide us with a test case. It displays nine images of the Adoration of the Magi, eleven images of Christ on the Cross, five of the Madonna and Child, four of the Pietà, as well as a score of other scenes from the life of Christ, but not a single Gethsemane scene. We might also note that the visual emphasis on the life of Jesus in the most popular Jesus biography of Vincent's day, Ernest Renan's *La Vie de Jesus*, barely mentions Gethsemane at all in its 282 pages. Chapter 21 of the book simply notes that Jesus and his disciples:

> went to the Garden of Gethsemane, at the foot of the Mount of Olives, and sat down there. Overawing his friends by his inherent greatness, he watched and prayed. They were sleeping near him, when all at once an armed troop appeared bearing lighted torches.[2]

That is the full extent of the Gethsemane story in Renan, an author Vincent much admired.

Having chosen to paint a "Garden of Olives—with a blue and orange Christ figure," as he informs Theo, what resources did the Gospel accounts provide Vincent, what choices did he make among the stories, and what might have led him to his particular vision of the scene? The Gospel of Mark is likely the earliest of the accounts and is worth quoting at the outset. It tells us that following the Last Supper with his disciples, after singing together a hymn, they went out to the Mount of Olives." Mark continues:

> And they went to a place which was called Gethsemane; and he said to his disciples, "Sit here while I pray." And he took with him Peter and James and John, and began to be greatly distressed and troubled. And he said to them, "My soul is very sorrowful, even to death; remain here and watch." And going a little farther, he fell on the ground and prayed that, if it were possible, the hour might pass from him. And he said, "Abba, Father, all things are possible to thee; remove this cup from me; yet not what I will, but what thou wilt." And he came and found them sleeping, and he said to Peter, "Simon, are you asleep? Could you not watch one hour? Watch and pray that you may not enter into temptation; the spirit

2. Renan, *La Vie de Jesus*, 246.

indeed is willing, but the flesh is weak." And again he went away and prayed, saying the same words. And again he came and found them sleeping, for their eyes were very heavy; and they did not know what to answer him. And he came the third time, and said to them, "Are you still sleeping and taking your rest? It is enough; the hour has come; the Son of man is betrayed into the hands of sinners. Rise and let us be going; see, my betrayer is at hand." (Mark 14:26–42)

Mark's account continues with the arrival of Judas and a threatening "crowd with swords and clubs." Judas betrays the identity of Christ with a kiss, and one of those with Jesus cuts off the ear of "the slave of the high priest." Jesus is then led away to questioning and trials, torments, and death.

We should note that Jesus is here portrayed for the first time by Mark in the Gethsemane story as suffering distress or anxiety regarding his impending death. Searching for some precedent to Mark's emphasis upon a chosen one's pain and suffering, one might turn to any number of biblical psalms of suffering. Psalm 22, for example, attributed to King David, also an "anointed one," opens with the familiar words Christ is pictured as speaking from the cross, "My God, my God, why hast thou forsaken me," and describes the psalmist as crying out, being scorned, despised, mocked, pierced, and stripped naked. This description is easily applied to the whole of the passion story, from Gethsemane to the crucifixion.

Seeking interpretations of Mark's Gethsemane account, we might view it as a demonstration of the "two ways" theme in biblical wisdom literature. Jesus is seen as representing the "way of life" through watchfulness and obedience to the divine even in his distress, while the disciples demonstrate the "way of death" as they fail to watch, miss the meaning of the moment, and fall asleep even after repeated urgings from Jesus. This may also agree with Mark's general theme that the disciples failed Jesus throughout his ministry. The account in Mark, followed by Matthew, not only finds the disciples failing all three opportunities to "watch and pray," but is remarkable in that Jesus' fervent prayer after throwing himself on the ground, receives no answer at all from God. The silence of God, an absence rather than a divine presence, permeates the story.

The symbol of a cup in the words attributed to Jesus at Gethsemane, "remove this cup from me," raises a variety of questions. The "cup of God's wrath" is a theme in the Hebrew prophets, a "cup of reeling" that causes one to fall as when intoxicated (Isaiah 51:17). But there is also a "cup of consolation" (Jeremiah 16:7) or the overflowing cup of God's care in Psalm

23:5. The many biblical references to cup include the "cup of the Lord" as opposed to the "cup of demons" in Paul (1 Corinthians 10:16–21) and Jesus' question to disciples, "Are you able to drink the cup that I am to drink?" (Matthew 20:22). The indication is that the cup Jesus asks to have removed includes the future events of suffering and death. When the "cup" word is followed by "yet not what I will but what you will," acceptance of such suffering and death are indicated, an obedience that will further the petition in the Lord's Prayer, that God's will "be done on earth as it is in heaven" (Matthew 6:10). Further, the reference to the cup serves to give substance to the preceding Gospel account of the Last Supper, where Jesus shares a cup with his disciples, announcing, "This is my blood of the covenant, which is poured out for many."

The account in the Gospel of Matthew (26:36–47), likely based upon the account in Mark, differs only slightly so far as wording and narrative are concerned. But Matthew's account does add words from Jesus responding to one of his group drawing a sword, "Do you think I cannot appeal to my Father, and he will at once send me more than twelve legions of angels?" (26:53). Luke omits reference to Gethsemane, referring rather to a "place" at the "Mount of Olives." He appears to condense Mark's account, with Jesus finding the disciples sleeping only once, removing some of the emphasis on their failure to support him. Further, Luke's Gospel has added two unique verses that place a special focus on the scene. Those two verses are not in some of the early manuscripts, and many scholars believe they were a later addition to Luke:

> And there appeared to him an angel from heaven, strengthening him. And being in an agony he prayed all the more earnestly; and his sweat became like great drops of blood falling down upon the ground. (Luke 22:43–44)

Likely the reference to "legions of angels" available to Jesus according to the Gospel of Matthew became incarnate in this tradition as the one "strengthening" angel of the Gospel of Luke. Further, the Greek words *en agonia* appear for the first time in the account, the only use in the New Testament, leading to the scene being described later as "Jesus' agony in the Garden." The seriousness of this *agon* (struggle, contest) was emphasized in this passage by the sweat that fell from Jesus' body to the earth "like great drops of blood." Some artists would later interpret this sweat as being actual blood of the savior, and so could paint the angel collecting Jesus' blood in a chalice.

Vincent's destroyed painting that he describes as "A Garden of Olives—with a blue and orange Christ figure, a yellow angel" gives precedence to the account in Luke with its description of "an angel from heaven strengthening him." This well suits Vincent's favoring of Luke's Gospel above most books of the Bible. Vincent wrote his young friend, the artist Emile Bernard, on June 26, 1888, that "Christian literature as a whole would certainly infuriate him (Christ), apart from Luke's Gospel, Paul's Epistles." Vincent went on to cite for Bernard a theme in early Christian tradition regarding Luke: "The patron saint of painters—St Luke—physician, painter, evangelist—having for his symbol—alas—nothing but the ox—is there to give us hope" (Letter 632). We will soon see that Vincent was not the only artist to turn to the Gethsemane or Mount of Olives story in Luke for inspiration, and it may be that angelic aid in time of personal agony became symbolic for some nineteenth-century artists of their own struggle and their hope of encouragement from some invisible realm. Certainly for Vincent, the choice of the Gethsemane event for his ghost paintings was the result of some deep urging, and for us it is a mystery calling for attention. Hopefully it will offer a glimpse into the artist's spiritual quest.

6

Agony and the Angel at Gethsemane

What was Vincent's own response to the Gethsemane scene and its role in the biblical drama? We will begin by examining Vincent's own use of the word "Gethsemane," a word found only twice in the entire Bible, but a number of times in the letters the artist wrote. Though both the Bible and the artist can also use "Garden of Olives" to refer to the Gethsemane site, we will most often focus on the term "Gethsemane" ("place of the olive-press") itself, as it becomes Vincent's favored term for that site of Christ's agonized prayer and betrayal.

A study of Vincent's references to the Gethsemane event makes clear that another source for his view of Jesus in Gethsemane existed alongside the Bible. The Bible as resource was accompanied, and perhaps at times dominated, by the visual resource provided by paintings and prints interpreting the Gethsemane scene. We might say that Vincent's letters indicate that his devotional reading of the Bible was paralleled by his devotional viewing of paintings. In most towns and cities he visited, fine arts museums attracted and claimed his enthusiastic attention. He described with care the paintings that most moved him, often in amazing detail. Even years after seeing a painting, it might continue to inspire him, and his visual memory appears to have been phenomenal, though not always totally accurate. As the following references in his letters will indicate, Gethsemane in the biblical stories he read and Gethsemane in the paintings he viewed likely merged or entered into conversation with each other in his imagination. He could see the biblical story through the interpretations of artists, and the interpretations of artists through his knowledge of the Bible.

Nineteen letters or related materials written by Vincent (including a sheet of biblical quotations and an incomplete, un-mailed letter) are specifically relevant to our search. Nine of the items refer specifically to paintings or to prints by artists other than Vincent himself. These nine include references to works by two of Vincent's friends, the artists Paul Gauguin and Emile Bernard. Three of the total nineteen references are the passages quoted earlier in our work, Vincent's descriptions of the paintings of Gethsemane he created and destroyed. Finally, there are references in his letters of 1889, written at the asylum in Saint Rémy and one reference in a letter written close to the time of his death from the village of Auvers-sur-Oise to Paul Gauguin, but never mailed.

The very first reference to "Gethsemane" is in a letter of May 31, 1875, to brother Theo. Vincent had just been transferred to Goupil's Paris branch at 9 rue Choptal, and was rooming in a house in Montmartre. He appears to have already begun to take advantage of the art resources of Paris. He wrote: "Yesterday I saw the Corot exhibition. It included a painting of the *Mount of Olives*; I'm glad he painted that" (Letter 34). Vincent then described for Theo the "olive trees, dark against the darkening blue sky" and the "background hills," with above them "the evening star." Vincent must have seen this work and over two hundred other Corot paintings in a retrospective Corot exhibition at the Ecole Nationale des Beaux-Arts.

Vincent's second reference to the Gethsemane event is in a letter written from Paris about five months later, October 11, 1875. In that letter (Letter 55) he writes Theo "to tell you in detail about my life here." He describes taking a new friend named Harry Gladwell to the Luxemberg Museum to show him "the paintings I like best there." Among the nineteen works he names are Hebert's *Christ on the Mount of Olives*, an image of Jesus in a white robe illuminated by lanterns, standing in the midst of a crowd that includes Judas, who is betraying him with a kiss.

From these two examples of references to the Gethsemane scene at the Mount of Olives, it is already becoming clear that Gethsemane itself contains a complex of themes and possible manners of presentation with quite different emphases. Corot views the image of Jesus alone in prayer enclosed by a dark, mysterious landscape, with perhaps one guiding star above. Hebert's painting focuses on the dominating image of Jesus, standing erect and illuminated, among those who betray and threaten his life.

Further references by Vincent to Christ in Gethsemane in religious art include prints of Christ in the Garden of Olives based on a work by the popular French artist Paul Delaroche, and *Christ in Gethsemane* by Ary Scheffer of Dordrecht in the Netherlands, the town where Vincent worked briefly for a bookseller. Writing to Theo on June 17, 1876 (Letter 84), Vincent described a print he had seen on the wall of their sister Anna's room. It was a print based on Paul Delaroche's *Christ in the Garden of Olives* depicting Jesus kneeling on rocky ground, his arms extended as he prays, his right hand closing around a chalice, the "cup" that he accepts. The Ary Scheffer painting of Gethsemane is mentioned in a letter of January 21, 1877, the first of Vincent's letters to Theo from Dordrecht in the Netherlands. Apparently Vincent's family preferred that he return from his work for a Methodist minister in England, at minimal recompense, and work in the Blussé and Van Braam bookshop in Dordrecht, at a regular wage. This first letter from Dordrecht indicates that Vincent's passion for biblical religion continued at its height. It is a confusing labyrinth of Scripture, prayers, hymns, and poems, likely reflecting the labyrinth of his own mind, filled with hopes of becoming a pastor or missionary, but equally filled with anxieties regarding the obstacles to his succeeding in that task. In the midst of his biblical quotations, hymns, and prayers, he informs Theo:

> The two prints of Christus Consolator that I got from you are hanging in my little room—saw the paintings in the museum, and also "Christ in Gethsemane" by Scheffer, which is unforgettable, a long time ago that painting moved Pa just as much. (Letter 101)

Ary Scheffer was an artist from Dordrecht whose statue was in view of the shop where Vincent worked. Prints of his *Christ the Consoler* (1837) and *Christ the Rewarder* (1848) would from then on regularly hang on the walls of Vincent's rented rooms. The *Consoler* print became Vincent's favorite, a seated Christ surrounded by persons representing all forms of suffering and sorrow, Christ's own pierced hands reaching out to heal and comfort them. The *Christ in Gethsemane* painting was apparently not available as a print, but Vincent saw the painting, and later took Theo to see it, at the Dordrecht Museum. Christ in profile is kneeling in a cave-like space, his eyes closed in prayer, his arms extended to the right, one hand reaching to a cup. A phantom-like angel extends over him, leaning over Jesus' head to comfort or protect. The fact that Theo had given Vincent the Consoler print, his father's having been moved by the Gethsemane painting, and Vincent's own visits to see the works at the museum during this period of religious enthusiasm must have sealed the importance of these works in Vincent's religious imagination. From here on in his letters, he will refer to the *Consoler* print he hangs in his rooms over twenty times.[1]

Among other references to Gethsemane is Vincent's handwritten copy of the Gethsemane story in Dutch from the Gospel of Luke. The copy begins with the opening words of the story in Luke, "And He came out, and went as He was wont, to the Mount of Olives," continuing through Jesus' admonition to his disciples to pray, and Jesus' own kneeling and prayer, "if Thou be willing, remove this cup from me! Nevertheless not my will but Thy will be done." It continues with the appearance of an angel "strengthening Him," Jesus' "agony" and sweat "as it were great drops of blood." The copy ends with the description of Jesus rising from prayer and finding the disciples "sleeping for sorrow." Vincent omits the following verses describing Judas' kiss, a slave's ear being cut and healed, and Jesus being seized and led away. *Vincent Van Gogh—The Letters* has placed the sheet among the "Related Manuscripts" on pages 301–26 of volume 5 (RM 10, page 310). The suggestion is that it was done in February or March of 1877 while Vincent worked in Dordrecht before moving to Amsterdam to be tutored in hopes of entering a university theology program.

The next reference to Gethsemane appears in Vincent's letter seeking to persuade Theo to obey their father in the matter of a woman Theo was seeing, whom Pastor Van Gogh considered of "low social standing." Not only does this one letter (104) contain eighty-nine quotations or allusions to some twenty-six books of the Bible, but it weaves those quotations together with hymns, poetry, and a long, rambling prayer "to Thee, O Christus Consolator" who makes us "thoroughly sorrowful yet always rejoicing." In that prayer, Vincent writes, "We also love Thy dark words: 'those which sat in darkness and in the shadow of death saw great light,' in their mind's eye Jesus Christ, and him crucified and Him in Gethsemane." Here, for the first time, Vincent clearly binds crucifixion and Gethsemane together, both to be conjured in the "mind's eye" of the struggling believer, apparently imitating Christ's Gethsemane through his own spiritual struggle. The agony of the "sorrowful" believer and the agony of Christ that led through Gethsemane to his crucifixion are linked and are described as the "dark words" of the Bible.

1. Chapter 12 of my book *Mystery of the Night Café* focuses on Ary Scheffer's image of Christ and its continuing importance to Vincent.

A further reference to Gethsemane occurs in a letter of May 31, 1877 (Letter 118). With the help of his father and his uncles, Vincent has left his employment in Dordrecht and moved to Amsterdam to prepare for the difficult entrance examinations that might allow him to study theology at the University of Amsterdam, and become an ordained Dutch Reformed minister. Later he will describe this period of intensive tutoring in Latin, Greek, history, and mathematics as the "worst time" of his life. The letter of May 31 to Theo contains long passages Vincent copied from a book on Dutch history as well as allusions to the Bible, including a reference to Gethsemane. Vincent writes, "It is also good to believe that, just as in olden days, now, too, an angel is not far from those who feel godly sorrow." Vincent then recounts the trials and tribulations of Elijah he has been reading in the Bible's Books of Kings, and of the "still small voice" through which God both encouraged and commanded Elijah to do his spiritual duty. He continues:

> And that story does not stand alone, we read of the Angel who strengthened Him in Gethsemane, who was sorrowful, even unto death, of the Angel who woke Peter from his sleep in prison, of the Angel who appeared to Paul in the night and said, "Fear not." And we, although we saw no Angel, although we are not the same as those men of old, should we not know that there is strengthening from Above?

Here the Gethsemane angel is related to stories in the book of Acts where an angel frees Peter from prison (Acts 12:7) and the Lord speaks in a "night vision" to Paul (Acts 18:9). Vincent had begun the study of Greek and almost certainly knew that the word for "angel" in the New Testament Greek (angelos) had the broader meaning of "messenger." So it appears that he can allow a merging of the sense of divine messages and the image of an actual heavenly being sent from God. The "still small voice" to Elijah, the "night vision" to Paul, the angels in Gethsemane, and as visitor to Peter in prison are closely related in his mind. But it is interesting that he can also imagine a boundary between the actual vision of an "angel" to "the men of old" and our knowing that "there is strengthening from Above." Did Vincent have a firm sense that visions of angels no longer occurred as "we are not the same as the men of old?" Did Vincent, for whom the visual was so important, hope, nevertheless, to have his own visions of angels? Are such visions a function of the imagination, and of the expectations of a particular era? These are questions we should keep in mind as we continue our search.

A letter of November 16, 1878, returns to the subject of the Geth-semane image in paintings or prints. By the spring of 1878, Vincent had given up his preparation for theological school as an impractical goal. With his father's help, he enrolled in a Flemish training college for evan-gelists near the city of Brussels. He began a three-month trial period late in August. A letter of November 16, 1878, to Theo from Laken, on the out-skirts of Brussels, tells of his hope to complete the training and become a preacher and teacher among the poor miners in the Belgian Borinage region. He enclosed a sketch of a worker's café where coal was sold, "Café Au charbonnages," in his letter, noting that he liked doing such sketches but that he would desist, as "it would most likely keep me from my real work." He describes some of the art that has moved him in the past, and asks Theo:

> Have you ever seen a painting, or rather a photo of it, by Carlo Dolci, *The Garden of Olives*? There's something Rembrandtesque about it, saw it recently. You no doubt know the large, rough etch-ing of the same subject after Rembrandt. . . . It came to mind after you told me that you had seen the painting by *père* Corot of the same subject; I saw it at the exhibition of his work shortly after he died, and it moved me deeply. (Letter 148)

The Dolci *Christ in Gethsemane* (no longer believed to be by Dolci), pictures Christ in a crimson robe kneeling with head bowed, and hands crossed on his chest. An angel approaches him holding a chalice and a cross.

The Rembrandt etching Vincent had come to mind is a dark scene with rays of light focused on an angel embracing Christ. The Christ figure kneels on the rocky ground, his eyes closed and his face lowered. Sleeping disciples are seen nearby, and a crowd is seen entering the area through a gate in the background. The fact that Vincent's favorite Dutch artist did an etching of Christ and an angel may have suggested to Vincent that Rembrandt had the privilege of access to such visions. It might further be suggested that even Rembrandt viewed such visions as taking place in the inner imagination. Christ's eyes are closed and his face lowered as he expe-riences the angel holding and comforting him.

About that time Vincent wrote that he would soon "try the Borinage plan." His schooling, even in the Belgian college for evangelists, had ap-parently not gone well, and difficult decisions regarding his life work had to be made. It is such a difficult moment of decision that may well bring Gethsemane to Vincent's mind. He was not, in fact, approved by the Bel-gian school, but by December of 1878 went to the Borinage on his own initiative. In January of 1879 he was approved on three-month probation to serve as a lay preacher, but at the end of the period he was dismissed. This was a dark time. Vincent refused to leave the Borinage, living in poverty among the families of miners. His father, apparently, considered having him declared incompetent and taken to Geel and its psychiatric hospital against his will. Brother Theo appears to have given up on his older brother, and they did not correspond again for a year. By February of 1881, Vincent had turned to art and Theo took upon himself the support of Vincent as an artist among laborers and peasants. After a stormy time practicing his art while living in the parsonage of his father and mother, Vincent left home and set up a studio in The Hague. It is then that he gathered a small family around himself, Sien (Clasina Hoornik), an ill prostitute, and her two children. But this arrangement embarrassed the Van Gogh family and friends, financial and personal problems multiplied, and failure seemed inevitable.

Two references to Gethsemane are found in letters from this period. Vincent had been living and working at his art in The Hague for almost two years, and family relations and financial problems had become a heavy burden. Earlier, we noted these two letters, one in which Vincent in deep discouragement writes that "my own future is a cup that cannot pass away except I drink," and the other is his description of the contrast between a Garden of Paradise ("Paradou") and the Garden of Gethsemane (Letter 374 and 381). The need for him to leave The Hague and Sien and her children is at the heart of his struggle in both these letters. Sien has apparently been planning to return to the streets, as her mother may have urged her, while Theo had made clear that he could not support both Vincent's art and his living with the woman. Vincent's letter of August 17 describes his love for that strange little family and his anguish at having to choose between his love for them and his duty toward his art. He writes, "There is no greater anguish than an inner struggle between duty and love." He affirms that "the wound" will remain with him forever. At that juncture, words from the Gethsemane story come to him. He writes that his "future is a cup that cannot pass away from me except I drink it." He follows with the conclusion of Jesus' declaration in Gethsemane, as well as in the Lord's Prayer: "So Thy will be done." A letter of September 5 continues his struggle regarding the necessity of his separation from the woman. He tells Theo that he has gone out in a rainstorm to "talk to nature," and has come to understand the meaning of being "gripped by true sorrow, moved by a calamity." That is when he writes the words: "Yes, for me the drama of a storm in nature,

the drama of sorrow in life, is the best. A 'paradou' is beautiful, but Gethsemane is more beautiful still" (Letter 381). The tension between apparent
opposites, the Garden of Eden and The Garden of Gethsemane, innocent
happiness and deep suffering, emerges as a central theme in Vincent's view
of the art of life itself. Echoed in letter after letter, it is clear that for Vincent
the way of deep sorrow is to be preferred, for it encloses within itself a
movement toward repentance, a transformation that embraces rather than
excludes joy. The "coincidence of opposites," or embracing of "antitheses"
was the very biblical context of Vincent's favorite words describing the
depth of life in a fractured world. The words reveal two forces seen clashing
in the Apostle Paul's view of the believer's struggle toward salvation. Two
antithetic perspectives are in tension, as the Apostle's letter makes clear:

> In honor and dishonor, in ill repute and good repute. We are treat-
> ed as impostors, and yet are true; as unknown, and yet well known;
> as dying, and behold we live; as punished, and yet not killed; as
> sorrowful, yet always rejoicing; as poor, yet making many rich;
> as having nothing, and yet possessing everything. (2 Corinthians
> 6:8–10)

A final series of references to Gethsemane in Vincent's letters fall
within his last three years of life. That includes letters from his most productive year, 1888, one from the Arles hospital in 1889, others from his year
of self-imposed "exile" during 1889 in an asylum in Saint Rémy, and one
unfinished letter of 1890 to Gauguin from the village of Auvers-sur-Oise
north of Paris.

Prior to his going to the south of France, Vincent had left Sien and
The Hague for a few months of homeless wandering in the rain and cold
of a bleak Drenthe landscape that brought moments of beauty and dark
times of depression. Ill and troubled, he returned to his father and mother
at the family parsonage, now in the town of Nuenen. His two years back in
Holland were marked by his father's sudden death, his painting of Zola's
novel *La Joie de vivre* beside his father's Bible, and his first "masterpiece,"
The Potato Eaters. Leaving home forever in 1886, he moved first to Antwerp and then to Theo's apartment in Paris. After two years of exciting
but exhausting interaction with the Impressionists of Paris, Vincent left to
recover in the sun of Provence, ill, suffering from heavy drinking and a cold
Paris winter. The year 1888 would be the apex of his brief life as artist, with
scores of canvases of blossoming trees, gardens, wild-flowers, fishing boats
on the Mediterranean, portraits of peasants, wheatfields and sunflowers.

Renting the "Yellow House," he hoped for a "monastery" to serve as a refuge for struggling artists, and encouraged Gauguin to come as its "abbot." By December of 1888 he had suffered a serious illness, cut a portion of his ear, and been hospitalized in serious condition. Gauguin had left, and the idea of a refuge for poor artists at the Yellow House had failed. He would be in and out of a hospital and an asylum for much of the rest of the days left to him, but not without a continuing body of amazing paintings and drawings.

Three of the references during 1888 are the descriptions of his two Gethsemane paintings and their destruction, as written in letters to Theo (Letters 637, 685) and to Emile Bernard (Letter 698). In a later chapter we will turn to a description of the context of those creations and destructions. Another reference of 1888 is in a letter to his youngest sister Wilhelmina, or Wil. She was then visiting with Theo in Paris, and Vincent was excited to learn what she thought of the art she was seeing. He asked her opinion of "Monticelli's bouquet of flowers that's at Theo's." Vincent made clear his own enthusiasm for Monticelli as a man and as a painter of the south: "I myself think about Monticelli a great deal down here. He was a strong man—a little, even very, cracked—dreaming of sunshine and love and gaiety, but always frustrated by poverty" (Letter 670). Vincent went on to recount: "He died in Marseille, rather sadly and probably after going through a real Gethsemane. Ah well, I myself am sure that I'll carry him on here as if I were his son or his brother."

Vincent's reference to Monticelli's "real Gethsemane" makes clear that the word "Gethsemane" itself could conjure up a life of poverty and suffering, as Monticelli was known to have had a series of strokes and very difficult days at the end of his life, with minimal support or recognition. In May of 1889, before leaving a hospital ward for the asylum, Vincent wrote sister Wil again, having heard she was nursing a woman suffering from cancer. He wrote, "you're very brave, my sister, not to recoil before these Gethsemanes" (Letter 764). Such agonizing "Gethsemanes" were likely in Vincent's mind as he thought of the very future of his own illness, as well as his choice to remain a painter among the poor.

Vincent's final references to Gethsemane include three written from the asylum at Saint Rémy and one from the village of Auvers-sur-Oise where he finally moved to be near his brother in Paris. Brother Theo had married, and Vincent wanted to move north again, be near Theo, and meet Theo's wife Johanna and the new child they had named after him. Vincent would live his final seventy days in that village north of Paris and would be buried in its graveyard. Before his suicide in a field of wheat, Vincent had begun writing a letter to his friend Paul Gauguin, a letter he never finished, and that letter contains his last reference to Gethsemane.

Through those final four references to Gethsemane, we become witnesses to a serious difference of opinion between Vincent and his two painter-friends Emile Bernard and Paul Gauguin regarding biblical paintings and the future direction of art. At the heart of the controversy are paintings of Christ in Gethsemane. We will turn to that clash of opinions and its significance after a chapter devoted to Vincent's own biblical painting, Jesus and the angel in Gethsemane. Our hope is to find clues in the events surrounding that twice-painted scene that will move us toward a solution to the artist's destruction of the works. My intuition is that those clues will take us more deeply than ever into the mind and work, the life and death, the sorrows and joys of Vincent van Gogh.

7

Vincent in Arles

Vincent had a radically sacramental view of nature, both in its heights and its depths, moments of ecstasy and moments of suffering. He had come south from the dark skies and storms of his home near the North Sea on a pilgrimage. Paris was a way-station, allowing him to reconnect with his brother Theo and to learn from the new movement in art called Impressionism. But life in a city was not for Vincent, and his hope was to discover in Provence what it was that the sun of the Mediterranean world had taught his painter-saints, Delacroix and Monticelli. He already knew the power of the darkness his homeland-saint Rembrandt had mastered. Even the lesser Dutch artists of The Hague School Vincent knew so well, Jozeph Israels and his own cousin Anton Mauve among them, had taught him a good deal about suffering and death among a people who struggled with the sea for land and a living. The titles of some of the popular paintings of Jozeph Israels are enough to indicate the trials and sufferings of the life of peasants and fishermen of Holland that must have caught Vincent's visual attention and weighed on his mind. Israels painted such works as *The Frugal Meal, In the Orphanage, Passing Mother's Grave, Fishermen Carrying a Drowned Man, Alone in the World,* and *Gleaning Potatoes.*

Once in Paris, Vincent saw the brilliant colors and focus on the recreations of ordinary people as painted by the Impressionists. But these scenes did not hold his attention for long. A need for the healing countryside and especially the Mediterranean sun he saw in the works of some of his favorite artists drew him south. Monticelli had painted in Marseille on the Mediterranean, and Marseille was called the "Gate of the Orient," suggesting the bright Japanese scenes the Van Gogh brothers were collecting. Delacroix painted in that same sun, just across the sea in North Africa. And so Vincent determined to leave the relative safety and care afforded by his brother Theo and their Montmartre apartment for the exciting new surroundings but isolation of the countryside around the old city of Arles. It was a pilgrimage that both confirmed and extended the coincidence of opposites, the antitheses that pulled Vincent's consciousness and artistic adventure taut. His roots in the darkness of storms along the North Sea would be illuminated by the Mediterranean sun, and his wish for a cooperative of artists would be tested by his solitude in Arles.

Vincent van Gogh boarded a train in Paris on February 19, 1888, after spending two years with his brother Theo in the great art center of the world of their day. The night train traveled the nearly five hundred miles south, the Route of the Sun, to Tarascon in Provence in some sixteen hours. Vincent transferred to a local train in Tarascon and arrived in the Arles Railroad Station. He would, as we noted earlier, remain in Arles and its countryside for 444 days, during which he would create two hundred paintings, over one hundred drawings and watercolors, and would write over two hundred letters. Thanks largely to brother Theo, his youngest sister Wilhelmina (Wil), and the young French artist Emile Bernard, those fascinating letters telling the story of his Arles pilgrimage were preserved and are available for our reading.

When Vincent arrived that February day, he was surprised that there were several inches of snow on the ground. Anxious to paint, he was soon hiking outside the city and painting a *Landscape with Snow*. He picked a sprig of almond blossom and placed it in a glass of water and painted it twice. By early March he was painting washerwomen at a bridge, and a tree-lined avenue with a train on the overpass by the railway station. What he saw brought to his mind the Japanese prints he and Theo had been collecting. He wrote Bernard about the middle of March:

> I want to begin by telling you that this part of the world seems to
> me as beautiful as Japan for the clearness of the atmosphere and
> the gay colour effects. The stretches of water make patches of a
> beautiful emerald and a rich blue in the landscapes, as we see it in
> the Japanese prints. (Letter 587)

On my own most recent trip to Arles, I chose the morning train from Paris to Arles, and so could marvel at the increasing strength of the sun and clarity of the atmosphere as I passed fields of ripening wheat, rows of sycamores, and the many small villages with red-tile roofs gleaming, most often gathered around a church tower. Before long an occasional field filled with sunflowers, a flock of sheep, vineyards, or olive groves were framed by my passenger-car window. By mid-afternoon I had arrived in the Arles Station. Arles is, for me, one of the most fascinating little cities in the world. In Vincent's day it had some twenty-three thousand inhabitants, with himself as likely the only Dutchman. Today there is a population of just over fifty thousand living among the Roman ruins, a famous ancient burial ground, narrow medieval streets, and a surrounding countryside filled with fruit-tree orchards, olive groves, fields of wheat and rice, and the scent of hill-sides covered with lavender.

I am particularly drawn to Arles, of course, because of my years of interest in the life and work of Vincent van Gogh. It is the one place in the world where I can most feel that I am walking the same winding stone streets Vincent walked, hiking the very fields and orchards he hiked, and very likely passing descendants of families that saw and wondered at the sight of that strange Dutchman loaded with wet canvases and painting gear. My guess is that at his early morning arrival, Vincent noticed the impressive sweep of the Rhone River, visible as one leaves the train station. He walked from the station through the railroad neighborhood with its laborers' cafés and its rooming houses. When I was there I passed through this same landscape on my way into the city known as the Porte de Cavalerie, the northern entrance to the city with its brownstone portals. The neighborhood outside the Portal, the Place Lamartine, was where Vincent finally rented a room over the Café de la Gare managed by Joseph and Marie Ginoux. Vincent painted the ground floor café he called "le café de nuit," the night café, with Joseph standing beside the billiard table. Marie Ginoux later came to the Yellow House at the other end of that same block to be painted by both Vincent and Paul Gauguin. Not far behind his Yellow House was the home of the bearded postal worker, Joseph Roulin, his wife Augustine, and their children. Roulin befriended Vincent, and the artist painted everyone in the family. One of the high points of Vincent's life was his decoration of the Yellow House, that section of a building he rented and transformed into a "real artist's house," with paintings of sunflowers and gardens. It was there that

Gauguin would join him for two months, and there that Vincent almost bled to death after cutting off a portion of his left ear.

I must at least note that I am disturbed that Vincent's neighborhood in Arles, where trains still rumble to the station and laborers' cafés still survive in spite of the loss of some buildings in a World War II bombing, is being erased from the tourist maps of Arles. The city authorities apparently favor sections of the city that have more lucrative shops and tourist attractions, like the areas around the forum and Roman Arena. Tourists, I found, are being misdirected, taken away from the north edge of the city where Vincent roomed at the Ginoux inn and decorated his Yellow House. A new "Van Gogh bedroom" has been constructed near the Arena while the forum's site of Vincent's *Café Terrace at Night* is now advertised as the "night café" where Vincent once lived and painted.

But let's enter the city itself, and see what Vincent would have seen. The old city is compact, and can be easily crossed by foot in thirty minutes. Around every corner of the narrow passageways there seems to be a surprise, some going back to the days when the Phoenician trading port was conquered by the Romans (123 BC) and later rewarded by Julius Caesar for siding with him against Pompey. Within fifteen minutes of walking its cobblestoned streets, one faces the impressive Roman arena and an expanse of shops and restaurants. Another brief walk takes one to the site of the old Roman Forum with its many outdoor restaurants and old hotels. One café terrace can be easily identified as the subject of a famous Van Gogh painting by gaslight. Another few minutes and one is at the Place de la République where women and children play by the fountain and old folks share the day's news. My guess is that Vincent was describing his experiences as he walked from his room at the north of the city to that very fountain when he wrote Theo:

> Must I tell you the truth and add that the Zouaves, the brothels, the adorable little Arlesiennes going off to make their first communion, the priest in his surplice who looks like a dangerous rhinoceros, the absinthe drinkers, also seem to me like creatures from another world? This doesn't mean I'd feel at home in an artistic world, but it means I prefer to make fun of myself than to feel lonely. (Letter 588)

On that open square is a small but impressive Romanesque church, St. Trophime. I can't help standing and gazing at its twelfth-century façade depicting the triumphant Christ surrounded by symbols of the gospel writers and vivid images of the torture of sinners and salvation of the saved. I know Vincent stood and studied that same façade, and so imagine what he thought of those stone carvings. We do have some clue of his mixed reaction. He wrote to Theo in that same letter:

> There's a Gothic porch here that I'm beginning to think is admirable, the porch of St. Trophime, but it's so cruel, so monstrous, like a Chinese nightmare, that even the beautiful monument in so grand a style seems to me to belong to another world, to which I'm so glad not to belong.

Just a few winding blocks southwest of St. Trophime I can enter the gateway to the old hospital where Vincent was taken when discovered bleeding in his bed on the morning of Monday, December 24, 1888, after his ear-cutting incident. The building is now called "l'éspace Van Gogh," and its courtyard with its flower-beds and fountain looks much as it did when Vincent, as a patient, painted it. A few blocks from the old hospital, I can take my choice of a bus to Saint-Maries-de-la-mer where Vincent painted the fishing boats, or in the opposite direction to Saint Rémy for a visit to his room in the asylum, or a hike through the fields and olive groves he painted beyond the asylum walls.

With these bits of background on the fascinations the city of Arles held for Vincent and continues to offers us, sights and experiences that may well allow us to feel his presence, let us turn specifically to the context of those two ghost paintings he created within months of his arrival. Those two paintings of Gethsemane will soon lead us to hike out into the countryside with Vincent to view the one site outside the city that most attracted his attention, a site he tells us he visited "fifty times," apparently never exhausting its mysterious appeal to his artist's eye and his feelings for the kinship of nature's offerings and the human quest.

8

Montmajour and the Two Gardens

On Sunday July 8 or Monday July 9 of 1888, Vincent wrote Theo from Arles that he had "scraped off . . . A Garden of Olives—with a blue and orange Christ figure, a yellow angel" (Letter 637). It had been 139 days since his arrival in Arles from Paris. We described his arriving to a landscape covered in snow, reminding him of Japanese prints he had seen. He began painting snow scenes and taking twigs of blossoms into his room to paint.

As March became April, and April became May, Vincent wrote his letters in the evenings, exhausted by long days in the sun painting apricot orchards, pink peach trees, blossoming almonds, and white pear trees. Those subjects were soon followed by irises, wheat fields, and farm houses with their gardens and wild flowers. His ecstatic state while painting in the orchards and fields is obvious. On April 3 he wrote, "I'm in a fury of work as the trees are in blossom and I wanted to do a Provence orchard of tremendous gaiety—writing to you in a calm frame of mind presents serious difficulties" (Letter 592). By April 9 he wrote Theo of his "rage to paint orchards," a "constant fever to work," and noted that Theo would "easily see that the pink peach trees were painted with a certain passion." On April 11 he described one of his "orchard" experiences:

> This morning I worked on an orchard of plum trees in blossom— suddenly a tremendous wind began to blow, an effect I'd only ever seen here—and came back again at intervals. In the intervals

sunshine made all the little white flowers sparkle. It was beautiful!
(Letter 595)

His almost frenzied brushwork in the excitement of painting the blossoming orchards is expressed in an April letter to Bernard:

> I follow no system of brushwork at all; I hit the canvas with irregular strokes which I leave as they are, impastos, uncovered spots of canvas—corners here and there left inevitably unfinished—reworking, roughnesses. (Letter 596)

As these few lines from his letters indicate, Vincent in Arles was himself being transformed by the coming of spring in the orchards. He was re-inventing himself as a painter of orchards and blossoming things, or perhaps better, was finding something deep inside himself that responded to the new life in nature under the Mediterranean sun.

By May, Vincent was painting the public gardens in his neighborhood near the railroad station, and hiking outside the city to paint wheatfields and irises, farmhouses, and wildflowers. June brought the new excitement of a trip by "diligence" to Les Saintes-Maries-de-la-Mer, where he spent several days painting and sketching the seaside village and its fishing boats on the Mediterranean. By mid-June he was surprised to find that in Provence it was already harvest time for hay and wheat, and he happily announced that he had become like any field laborer, working from dawn to dark.

July arrived, and we find ourselves with those letters closest to his announcement of the Gethsemane painting and its destruction. I begin with a letter a dozen days before he tells Theo of that "Jesus and the angel" painting, searching that letter for some clue to Vincent's "Gethsemane." On June 28, Vincent wrote Theo that he had completely "reworked" his painting of "the sower against a yellow and green sky with earth purple and orange" (Letter 634). Sowing the fields immediately followed the harvest, and so Vincent's very first attempts at art in the Borinage several years earlier, which focused on copying Millet's peasants harvesting, digging, and sowing, must have come to his mind along with the harvest scenes he was painting and the new sowing he observed. In his letter he compared paintings by two of his favorite artists, Delacroix's *Christ Asleep during the Tempest* in a fishing boat on the Sea of Galilee, and Millet's *Sower*. The Delacroix, Vincent affirmed, "speaks a symbolic language through color itself." He goes on to note that if you pursue such a language, "you fall into a whole metaphysics of colors à la Monticelli. . . . That makes you absent-minded like a sleep-walker." He then described his painting of the new iron Trinquetaille bridge over the Rhone, followed by the words, "One more effort that's far from finished—but one at least where I'm attempting something more heart broken and therefore more heartbreaking."

Vincent's description of Delacroix's Christ *Asleep during the Tempest* indicates that he was amazed by that Christ with a startling "lemon yellow halo." It calls to mind another Delacroix image of Christ that became a print Vincent cherished and hung in his room, Delacroix's *Pietà*, the body of Christ in the arms of his mother. When that print of the *Pietà* was accidently dropped into paint and ruined during a seizure later in the asylum in 1889, Vincent "copied" it, or interpreted it in color as a small oil painting he would keep in his rented rooms until his death. During that period of doing "copies" or "interpretations" of the works of other artists, he in fact copied three specifically religious works: Delacroix's *Pietà* and *Good Samaritan* and Rembrandt's *The Raising of Lazarus*. Only *Pietà* displays an image of Christ, as Vincent omits Christ from the Rembrandt, focusing instead upon Lazarus rising and the amazement of his two sisters at the opening of the cave-tomb. It appears that he places from memory two of his friends from Arles, Marie Ginoux and Augustine Roulin as Mary and Martha in the Rembrandt scene, and some see Lazarus as having a resemblance to Vincent himself. The *Good Samaritan* we might describe as Delacroix's illustration of Jesus' gospel of caring for the needs of the outcast, the gospel of Jesus embodied in a parable standing in for the image of Jesus himself. Those three paintings, from their various perspectives, use the work of favorite artists to "model" for Vincent's religious scenes, and seem intended especially for his own personal devotional life. Vincent choosing to paint Jesus in Gethsemane becomes all the more complicated when we add those three "copies" to his total work, placing them beside his personal choice of the Gethsemane scene.

Even among his copies of works by favorite artists, we see that Vincent included only one Christ figure, Delacroix's *Pietà*, and that was likely intended for his own personal use, replacing a print he had damaged. Have we here some clue to a deep level of Christ-devotion in Vincent's inner life that he kept to himself during his days as artist? Did there persist a fascination for Christ that began in his parsonage days and was later fed by his love of Thomas à Kempis' *Imitation of Christ* and the Ary Scheffer print of Christ the Consoler, given him at a critical time in his religious life by brother Theo?

Going back to our quotation from Vincent's June 28 letter, I have struggled with his words that follow his description of the bridge painting. Is it the bridge painting with its human figures that Vincent described in that letter as "one more effort . . . that is more heart broken and so more heart-breaking" or might he be describing the painting of Jesus in Gethsemane he would finish and then destroy? I have studied the facsimile of this two-page letter in hopes of getting some answer. The second page of the letter gets very cramped for space, and whether the gap between Vincent's reference to the bridge painting and reference to "one more effort" that is "heart-breaking" might be the first hint of his painting the Gethsemane scene remains a question for me. Shadows of persons at the bridge under an "absinthe" sky may well be described as heart-breaking, but the Gethsemane scene might be even more so. For me, the choice between these two possibilities remains an unresolved puzzle.

Whether Vincent was already hinting to Theo that he had a "Jesus and angel" painting, it is clear that on June 28 Vincent was thinking of the power of Delacroix's image of Christ lying in the storm-tossed fishing boat among his fearful disciples. That is not far from an antithetic play on the drama of Gethsemane, with Delacroix's Christ now sleeping and his fearful disciples imploring him to awaken in a storm. Gethsemane, in suggestive contrast, has the disciples sleeping and Christ the one in agony. We should also remind ourselves that Vincent associated storms in life with Gethsemane, and preferred the storms and the Garden of Gethsemane to a placid Garden of Paradise.

But it is Vincent's letter preceding his mention of the Gethsemane painting that intrigues me most, and may offer revealing clues to the painting's origins. In his letter of July 5 Vincent wrote to Theo:

> Yesterday at sunset, I was on a stony heath where very small, twisted oaks grow, in the background a ruin on the hill, and wheat-fields in the valley. It was romantic, it couldn't be more so, à la Monticelli, the sun was pouring its very yellow rays over the bushes and the ground, absolutely a shower of gold. And all the lines were beautiful, the whole scene had a charming nobility. (Letter 636)

In this passage, Vincent made clear how illuminating the experience was to him, but it may be that what he does not explain to Theo is even more important. What he describes as the "ruin on the hill" where this experience occurs, is actually Vincent's favorite site outside the city of Arles, the famous Abbey of Montmajour, a monastery founded in the sixth century and rebuilt in the eleventh and twelfth centuries. Might it be that Vincent's "shower of gold" on that rocky prominence in the shadow of that old Christian monastery put him in mind of his biblical heritage, such scenes as Moses on the mountain at the burning bush, or Elijah at his mountain cave hearing God's still small voice? Better yet, might that rocky prominence showered in gold conjure in his imagination the site of Jesus at Gethsemane met by a golden angel? We will see that he will sketch the olive trees he discovers there, as well as the nearby tangle of trees and vines he describes as a Paradou, a Garden of Paradise where he picks and eats figs. Is it here that the antithesis of the "two gardens" confronts him, moving him to choose and to paint Gethsemane rather than Paradise?

Vincent was one of his generation's most avid readers, who read with his "heart" as well as his head. His reading of the Bible, *Imitation of Christ*, all of Dickens, Zola, Balzac, Shakespeare, samplings from other great writers of France, Germany, and some of the works of Poe, Whitman, and Harriet Beecher Stowe in the United States enriched his own imagination and his own letters. My guess is the descriptions of the Holy Land he read in the Bible and in Ernest Renan's *The Life of Jesus* easily led Vincent to experience that rocky mount with its olive trees and monastery ruins as comparable to those interstices on earth that in biblical times opened the way to the deeper meaning of things. For Vincent this may have been a calling of prophets and artists to responsible choices illuminating a future of hope and comfort through a Gethsemane of labor and suffering.

This is, of course, a personal conjecture, and I admit I am led to it in part by my own experiences hiking to Montmajour in order to better understand Vincent's attraction to that mysterious ruin on the rocky crag north of Arles. Immediately at the east side of Vincent's Yellow House was Avenue de Montmajour. Passing under the railroad viaduct one hikes the avenue northward toward the ruin on the rocky mount, which is visible from a distance of some miles. Before long one is passing fields of wheat and rice, with dusty lanes giving access to old farmhouses. At a curve on a narrow road a tangle of trees covers the rocks that ascend to the monastery. On my visits, I was the only person there to climb the ruin's tower and view the countryside below. I entered the large, empty sanctuary listening to the echo of my own footsteps on the stone floor. I clambered over rocks to find hermit cells built into the monastery walls, and spent time at the mysterious cross-shaped chapel of the dead behind the monastery, surrounded by scores of empty sarcophagi carved into the natural rock. Flights of crows nested in the dead trees around the chapel and completed the awesome scene.

A day or two after the letter mentioning his Gethsemane painting, Vincent described for Theo another hike to Montmajour, this time with a friend named Milliet, a Zouave second lieutenant. Here the "Paradou" imagery predominates, but the monastery is a silent, effective presence:

> I've just come back from a day at Montmajour, and my friend the second lieutenant kept me company. So the two of us explored the old garden and we stole some excellent figs there. If it had been bigger it would have made you think of Zola's Paradou, tall reeds, grape vines, ivy, fig trees, olive trees, pomegranate trees with fat flowers of the brightest orange, hundred-year-old cypresses, ash trees and willow, rock oaks. Half demolished staircases, ruined Gothic windows, clumps of white rock covered in lichen, and pieces of collapsed wall scattered here and there in the undergrowth; I brought back another large drawing of it. (Letter 638)

Later in the letter he compares the color-merchant from Paris, Père Tanguy, "with the early Christian martyrs and slaves," and concludes his letter with musings on the meaning and destination of life itself: "That rakes up the eternal question: is life visible to us in its entirety, or before we die do we only know one hemisphere? . . . In the Life of the painter, death may perhaps not be the most difficult thing." Again, in my imagination, thoughts of the Garden of Paradise through a Zola novel's lens might well have been stirred in Vincent by a day among the fig trees, rocks, and holy ruins of Montmajour. They could easily embody Vincent's feeling for that ruined monastery and the ascetic monks who once sought their life direction there. Vincent himself would be inspired to make of his Yellow House a monastery for artists, with himself as a simple monk searching for the art of the future. Vincent would send his self-portrait as a monk to Gauguin, and invite Gauguin to be the Abbot leading the cause. Vincent's letter of July 10 was moved to compare the color merchant Tanguy to a "Christian martyr" and to describe Vincent as seeking some illumination of that hidden hemisphere of life-death. Such a search, such a personal Gethsemane, might well mean that for the artist in a confusing time of urbanization, industrialization, and the accompanying dislocations there were more difficult things for a pilgrim-monk-artist than death.

The importance of the Gethsemane-like setting at Montmajour as a catalyst to Vincent's generally hidden "biblical imagination" receives further emphasis when two months later he reported to Theo that he had repeated the painting and its destruction. He included a new reason for trying the painting again: "Because here I see real olive trees" (Letter 685). He would sketch those olive trees, as well as the rocky ledges and the monastery ruin. Later he would pick up the theme of olive groves and specifically associate such scenes with Gethsemane, as we will note later in his correspondence with the young artist Emile Bernard, who painted his own work on Jesus in Gethsemane.

Vincent's response to the Montmajour setting that led him to seek it out "fifty times" might well have made Arles his "holy city" and Montmajour his "holy mountain," a site for angelic illuminations. But such conjectures would be more convincing if that letter he wrote on July 5 recounting for Theo his experience of the "shower of gold" had some more direct mention of his contact with biblical language regarding Gethsemane.

Is there any such evidence in that letter? Yes, there is, through one of Vincent's most potent resources: reading novels. The letter of July 5 that immediately precedes the letter telling of the Gethsemane painting is four pages long. Interestingly enough, page three has a sketch of a "garden with a weeping tree," a sketch he made at the public gardens outside the Yellow House. That garden scene and weeping tree became a personal favorite of Vincent's and might itself be related to his thoughts of Gethsemane. The following page of his letter begins with a reference to the book he was currently reading. Here we have the passage on the garden sketch and the book being read: "Here's a new subject. A corner of a garden with round bushes and a weeping tree. . . . I'm reading Balzac, *César Birotteau*. I'll send it to you when I have finished it—I think I'll re-read all of Balzac." *César Birotteau* is Balzac's novel of an honest merchant who is brought from wealth to poverty through the dishonesty of others, the greed of money-lenders, and through certain laws dealing with bankruptcy and finance that hold César alone responsible. The story tells how César takes it upon himself through hard labor and sacrifice to repay all the debts owed, even beyond the law's requirements. His honor is restored at the end of the story, but his broken health leads to a crisis and his death. Well into the novel, César's spiritual director, a good priest, comes to him as he struggles with his losses. The priest, Abbé Loraux says to César:

> My son . . . your sentiments of submission to the Divine will have long been known to me, now you are called to put them into practice. Keep your eyes fixed ever upon the Cross, contemplate

the Cross without ceasing, and think of the cup of humiliation of which the Saviour of men was compelled to drink, think of the anguish of His Passion, and thus you may endure the mortification sent to you by God.[1]

Though Vincent did not generally put that same emphasis on the cross, especially in his later references to the Bible, the passage in Balzac likely stirred his own sense of sacrifice, and certainly points directly at Gethsemane, Jesus' agonizing, and the cup that he was called upon to accept as the divine will. Not only was Vincent sacrificing for a new art, but he must have identified with César in his own sense of guilt that he owed brother Theo so much more than he could ever repay. César is counseled to "imitate" Christ in drinking the cup of suffering and even death.

Near the end of the novel, César's sudden death that surprises and shocks those around him is also interpreted by the spiritual advisor, Abbé Loraux, in biblical images familiar to Vincent:

> "Behold the death of the righteous!" The Abbé Loraux said solemnly as he stretched his hand towards César with one of those Divine gestures which Rembrandt's inspiration beheld and recorded in his picture of Christ raising Lazarus from the dead. Christ bade Earth surrender her prey; the good priest sped a soul to heaven, where the martyr to commercial integrity should receive an unfading palm.[2]

Vincent, as we have noted, would copy the Rembrandt print described here, though omitting the Christ-figure and focusing on the resurrected Lazarus and his marveling sisters. It is noteworthy that Vincent would have read this reference in Balzac to Rembrandt as having seen Christ and his gesture through artistic inspiration. Perhaps Vincent considered such inspired visions as one of the mysterious gifts available to suffering artists. Perhaps Vincent saw, if not the cross of Christ, the comfort offered by the yellow light of an angel to that Galilean peasant who chose the agony of the Garden of Gethsemane over the pleasures of the Garden of Paradise.

1. Balzac, *César Birotteau*, 264.
2. Ibid., 323.

9

Rembrandt's Christ and Vincent's Quandary

Vincent was struggling with the direction his painting was taking. He saw it had not only left behind the historical themes and important personages that provided the subjects for many earlier painters, but was departing from the approach of the Impressionists he had counted as his teachers and colleagues in Paris. Was he returning to his early intent to become a peasant-painter like Millet, or was he discovering a new art of "suggestive color" that might lead beyond Delacroix and Monticelli toward painting as a "musical-abstraction"? Perhaps he was becoming a folk-painter of naïve country images, or a Dutchman in France painting a kind of Japanese nature mysticism. Was there in his art any place for the religious images that had fed his soul for so many years, from Dutch parsonage to Belgian mining villages? These questions take us to a series of letters he exchanged with his friend, the young French painter Emile Bernard. I noted in an earlier chapter that I had left some references to Gethsemane in Vincent's letters for a later examination, and that moment has come. Through his correspondence with Bernard, hidden aspects of Vincent's deepest imagination and theology emerge, aspects that eluded us in his letters to Theo. It may be that Vincent was finally so strident in his argument with Bernard regarding their differing views of the future of painting and its relationship to Christian themes that the sometimes petulant Bernard refused to correspond any further with Vincent. If so, that was a decision he likely regretted and sought to make amends for once Vincent had died.

Who was this Emile Bernard? From the point of view of Van Gogh letters, he is the young French "avant garde" artist who valued and saved the twenty-two letters Vincent sent to him between 1887 and 1889. He would be, in fact, the first to publish a collection of Vincent's letters. To Bernard we may owe the very impulse to make Vincent's letters available to the world. Those twenty-two letters begin with one Vincent sent to Bernard while both were painting in Paris and had just begun discussing art together after meeting at classes in the Paris painting-studio of Fernand Cormon. Bernard (1868–1941) was fifteen years younger than Vincent, and so was a precocious and apparently difficult teenager when they first met.

Vincent's first letter apologizes for an angry exchange he had with Bernard, but Vincent goes on to attempt a gentle correction of Bernard's "sectarian" refusal to allow his paintings to hang in shows that contained any paintings by the pointillists (Letter 575). Another eighteen letters are exchanged with Bernard while Vincent is in Arles and Bernard is either painting in Paris or has gone to paint with Gauguin in Pont Aven (summer and fall 1888). The last of those eighteen is, in fact, to Bernard from both Vincent and Gauguin, during Gauguin's brief stay at the Yellow House in Arles. The final two letters to Bernard are sent by Vincent from the asylum in Saint Rémy. It appears that Bernard was offended by the final letter and cut off all correspondence. That letter is one of the most crucial bits of evidence in our Gethsemane search, as it deals directly with a Gethsemane painting by Bernard and Vincent's response to it.

All of Vincent's letters to Bernard are interesting, but three of them are far more than that; they are absolutely crucial to our understanding of Vincent's spirituality and relationship to traditional Christian imagery during his ten years as artist. A letter sent by Vincent from Arles on June 26, 1888, tells us more about his views as artist regarding the Bible and Jesus than all his letters to Theo from Arles, Saint Rémy, or Auvers. Another letter sent from Arles to Bernard about a month later (July 29) adds puzzling aspects of Vincent's views of images of Jesus painted by Rembrandt and Delacroix. Finally, Vincent's very last letter to Bernard over a year later, sent from the asylum at Saint Rémy on November 26 of 1889, gives us Vincent's very negative critique of the scenes from the life of Christ as painted by Bernard, including a Garden of Gethsemane painting. Further, Vincent provides there a preferred alternative approach to painting the Garden of Gethsemane. Vincent and Bernard never again corresponded, and Vincent would die in Auvers-sur-Oise north of Paris some 244 days after that last letter to Bernard.

The first of those three letters crucial to our understanding may well come as a complete surprise to anyone who has read the wealth of previous letters Vincent had written since becoming an artist. Who would have guessed that Vincent, having felt betrayed by Christian clergy and churches, would have continued to muse deeply on the nature of the Bible, the role of Christ in history, and the consolation of Jesus' preaching? But it is all suddenly expressed here in this letter to Bernard on Tuesday, June 26, 1888.

What is even more crucial for our search for the origin of the ghost paintings is the fact that Vincent's thoughts on the nature of Jesus' life and ministry are located in a letter written just nine days before he reports his moving experience at that "ruin on a hill," that "shower of gold" on a "stony heath." Further, we should note that this letter's enthusiasm for the life and intentions of Christ comes only thirteen days before his confession to Theo that he has painted and scraped off "A Garden of Olives—with a blue and orange Christ figure, a yellow angel." Vincent's letters to Theo from Arles gave no hint that a painting of Gethsemane was even a remote possibility, but this one letter to Bernard suddenly reveals a facet of Vincent's spiritual life as artist otherwise hidden from view. In the light of Vincent's correspondence with the young artist Bernard, a Van Gogh painting of Jesus in Gethsemane makes both religious and artistic sense. Its destruction may make equal sense and be equally revealing.

Vincent's letter of June 26 opens with these words: "You do very well to read the Bible—I start there because I've always refrained from recommending it to you" (Letter 632). In the lost correspondence of Bernard to Vincent, Bernard must have initiated the subject of the Bible and opened the gate to Vincent's passionately held views on the developmental nature of the Bible, the relative value of New Testament books, the heart of Jesus' preaching, and the relation of all this to the life of the modern artist. Is this an oblique admission that Vincent's letters to his brother Theo had purposely avoided such subjects? My guess is that this is so. Vincent, once he became an artist, awaited an invitation to engage in views on Christian literature and thought before he would offer his perspective. He told Bernard that he had "always refrained" from recommending the Bible to him. I can imagine that Vincent felt embarrassed by the scores of letters he once sent to Theo and the Van Gogh family during his days reading the Bible in Paris, preaching for British Methodists, and studying with Dutch tutors in Bible and theology. The memory of those letters with their long disjointed prayers, scores of biblical quotations, evangelical admonitions, and extended passages from hymns and religious poetry must have seemed presumptuous and ill-advised to Vincent once he became an artist. Vincent would likely now carefully avoid all such rants. He would not speak of his deepest spiritual concerns and views on Bible and Jesus unless requested to do so.

Our consideration of the Vincent-Bernard correspondence on the subject of the Bible may call attention to what I believe is the elephant in the room of Van Gogh studies. What I have in mind are such questions as: What was the inner life of Theo van Gogh? What were the thoughts and attitudes that made up his character? What, in particular, were his sensitivities as older brother Vincent understood them and to some extent catered to them? What did Vincent feel free to discuss and what did he avoid in letters to his brother?

Allow me my best guess regarding Theo. I view Theo as a responsible and gentle Dutchman who had become a citizen of the great world-metropolis of culture and the arts—the city of Paris. He lived in a city that prided itself on its secular stance in the world. In my book *Mystery of the Night Café* I attempted a quick sketch of religion as viewed by many Parisians of that day. I quote there W. Scott Haine's book *The World of the Paris Café*. He notes that cafés could be described as the new churches for many in the city:

> The allusion to churches is especially apt, because the rise of the café after 1789 coincided not only with the decline in religious belief among the Parisian lower orders but also with a dramatic decline in the number of places of worship in the city. Of the 290 churches in Paris before the Revolution, more than 200 were later either sold as national properties or demolished.[1]

My guess is that Paris as an increasingly secular city both suited and formed the perspective of Theo. Within that secular city Theo associated largely with artists, viewed by many as socialists, anarchists, and most often atheists, and this may have further influenced his own secular views.

If my above guess is right, Vincent would likely have avoided the error of his past. He would leave the spiritual nature of his own continuing pilgrimage out of his correspondence with Theo. If Theo had raised questions of religious faith and practice, would Vincent have enthusiastically engaged in such a discussion? I believe so, but we have no such exchanges.

---

1. Haine, *The World of the Paris Café*, 3.

Jan Hulsker makes some attempt to face this elephant in the room through his "dual biography," *Vincent and Theo Van Gogh*, but even Hulsker's access to Van Gogh family letters does not provide a very complete inner-portrait of the man to whom Vincent wrote most of his letters. The future of Van Gogh studies may have much to do with learning more about the enigmatic Theo, whose view of life and whose sensitivities may determine much that Vincent addressed and much that he avoided in their correspondence.

We may have to search for texts that help us assess Theo's deepest thoughts and feelings. If I were suggesting one text as a test-case, I would turn to Theo's letter of distress when he and Johanna's child had suddenly become very ill and they felt they were in danger of losing him. Does the distraught Theo allude in any way to the hope for divine help? Does he ask his former evangelist-brother to pray for the baby Vincent, the artist's godchild? Does he ask Vincent to send a note of spiritual comfort to Johanna? No, he does not. He simply elaborates on the crisis in his home. Theo's letter of distress then goes on to discuss his hopes and fears regarding the future, and again, there is no reference to religious themes (Letter 894). All this may be a rather feeble bit of evidence for Theo's lack of any traditional religious concerns, but I am simply probing for clues. Perhaps the best evidence of Theo's lack of interest in traditional religious concerns is to be found in the wonderful collection of letters he exchanges with his wife-to-be, Johanna, in the collection titled *Brief Happiness: The Correspondence of Theo Van Gogh and Jo Bonger*. In that collection of intimate letters, not only are there no references to traditional religious themes or concerns, but it is interesting that one of the worries shared by Theo and Jo is that Theo's mother might be offended that they want no part of a church wedding. I hope we will one day learn more about Theo as a subject of interest in and of himself, but also as a way of assessing the life and thought of brother Vincent. After all, some 658 of Vincent's 819 letters were written to Theo.

Now we return to Vincent's letters to Emile Bernard. What does that letter of June 26, 1888 (Letter 632) tell us of Vincent's view of the life of Jesus, and so what light might it shine on the context within which he painted the Gethsemane scene? He begins by praising Bernard for reading the Bible, and then, likely with a smile, names such an interest in biblical texts "the artist's neurosis," admitting that he himself has long suffered from it. He goes on to express what one might call a "modernist-critical" view of the Bible and its development, colored by his own negative experiences.

He admits that much of the Bible: "Stirs up our despair and our indigna-
tion—thoroughly upsets us, completely outraged by its pettiness and its
contagious folly." But a consoling kernel, he notes, is found inside the Bible's
hard husk, and that kernel is Christ:

> Christ—alone—among all the philosophers, magicians, etc. de-
> clared eternal life—the endlessness of time, the non-existence of
> death—to be the principle certainty. The necessity and the *raison
> d'etre* of serenity and devotion. (Letter 632)

The meaning for Vincent of these rather vague and poetic descriptions of
Jesus' teachings have some kinship to the "transcendent timelessness" of
Christ as expressed in Renan's humanistic *Life of Jesus*. But Vincent's letter also focused on earthly illustrations of "transformation" that reveal the
"changed conditions of existence" we seek. He declares that transformation will be "no cleverer and no more surprising than the transformation
of the caterpillar into a butterfly." In Vincent's gospel of comfort, "Christ's
words concerning the other half of existence" will reveal life as "far superior
in extent and potentialities to the single hemisphere that's known to us at
present."

At the heart of Vincent's presentation of his view of Christ to Bernard
is the assertion that Christ:

> Lived serenely as an artist greater than all artists, disdaining mar-
> ble and clay and paint—working in LIVING FLESH. i.e.—this ex-
> traordinary artist, hardly conceivable with the obtuse instrument
> of our nervous and stupefied modern brains made neither statues
> nor paintings nor even books..... he states it loud and clear..he
> made..LIVING men, immortals. (Letter 632)

Vincent's focus on the "art" of Christ turns to Christ's spoken words, specifically the parables:

> This great artist—Christ—although he disdained writing books
> on ideas or feelings—was certainly much less disdainful of the
> spoken word—THE PARABLE above all. (What a sower, what a
> harvest, what a fig tree, etc.). (Letter 632)

Vincent concludes this description of Christ as artist by noting that "those
spoken words" are "one of the highest, the highest summit attained by art,
which in them becomes a creative force, a pure creative power."

Viewing Christ as an artist or a poet was not unique to Vincent, and
flourished among the Romantics, but Vincent's knowledge of the Bible,

Thomas à Kempis' *Imitation of Christ*, religious themes and figures in the novels of George Eliot, Charles Dickens, and others, enriched that image beyond his artist-peers. Even more exceptional was his personal application of Jesus' teachings to his life as preacher, evangelist, and willing servant among the poor. Further, Vincent's image of Jesus as artist was extended to include his description of God as artist and this world as his art work. On May 26, 1888, Vincent wrote Theo from Arles, expressing his concern that a doctor had warned Theo of a heart condition. Certainly Vincent intended some humor to cheer his younger brother, but the image he chose to explain the flaws in creation is daring, and matches his own struggles as artist:

> I'm thinking more and more that we shouldn't judge the Good Lord by this world, because it's one of his studies that turned out badly. But what of it, in failed studies—when you're really fond of the artist—you don't find much to criticize—you keep quiet. But we're within our rights to ask for something better. We'd have to see other works by the same hand though. This world was clearly cobbled together in haste, in one of those bad moments when its author no longer knew what he was doing, and didn't have his wits about him. (Letter 613)

Vincent went on in this passage to note that this world, a study "worked to death," a "mistake" nevertheless shows the trouble taken by the hand of a master artist, and so our consolation is that we can be in "hope of seeing better than that in another life." This description of the divine Creator's failed experiment may have some direct bearing on the experiments expected of any sincere artist. If so, perhaps we have here one explanation for Vincent's own experiment, likely a month or more later, his canvas of Christ and an angel in Gethsemane.

But let us return to Vincent's June 26 letter to Bernard (Letter 632). As to artists who have painted the image of Christ, Vincent tells Bernard: "The figure of Christ has been painted—as I feel it—only by Delacroix and by Rembrandt........And then Millet has painted....Christ's doctrine." Vincent went on to note that many others over the centuries had painted images of Christ, and often done so very well from a painterly perspective. But from a religious perspective, he sees all those beyond Delacroix and Rembrandt to be basically "pagans" in their ability to portray Christ effectively:

> The rest makes me smile a little—the rest of religious painting— from the religious point of view—not from the painting point of view. And the Italian primitives (Botticelli, say), the Flemish,

German primitives. . . . They're pagans, and only interest me for
the same reason that the Greeks do, and Velazquez, and so many
other naturalists.

What is it about the images of Christ in Delacroix and Rembrandt that so
moved Vincent religiously? We will return to that question, for Vincent
picks it up in a rather confusing letter to Bernard about a month later, on
July 29, 1888. But first, a brief but I believe significant note that has much
to say about our entire search for the ghost paintings.

Only after reading Vincent's correspondence from Arles over many
times did I notice that we may well have a truly "purloined letter" hidden
among his correspondence of the spring and summer of 1888. The unique-
ness of the letter we have just examined extends to the way it is printed
in the new six-volume set of letters published by the Van Gogh Museum.
Dots, dashes, words in capital letters, parentheses, and phrases in italics,
all occur in the section on Vincent's views regarding Jesus. I turned to van-
goghletters.org to view again the facsimile of letter 632 and found the reason. Unlike the letters before and after this one, Vincent's words here seem
scribbled wildly, some large, some small, some squeezed between previous
lines, some horizontal, some vertical, several scratched out and revised. It
is not that we never before saw Vincent doing some of these things, but the
concentration in the Jesus materials in this one letter is rather unique. In
my view, the very manner in which Vincent wrote his views of Jesus is a
revelation of his excitement in releasing feelings otherwise hidden. His very
"hand" demonstrates a high pitch of emotion. His use of the pen here, as
the use of his brush in his paintings, gives away his deep feelings. He writes
this letter as he paints: from the heart. It puts me in mind of the very way
he described for Bernard his manner of painting under the influence of the
blossoming trees on April 12:

> I follow no system of brushstroke at all; I hit the canvas with irreg-
> ular strokes which I leave as they are, impastos, uncovered spots
> of canvas—corners here and there left inevitably unfinished—re-
> workings, roughnesses. (Letter 596)

Vincent's own "thinking and feeling hand" has shaped both his excited engagement with an Arles' orchard in bloom and a host of hidden feelings
and thoughts regarding his spiritual search. The first page of this letter to
Bernard on June 26 (Letter 632) stands as a key piece of evidence regarding the significance his daring to paint Christ and an angel in Gethsemane
must have had, and his weighty decision to destroy the work.

We turn now to the second of the three letters to Bernard I have singled out as of special relevance, his letter of July 29, 1888. This letter includes his attempt to explain what he meant when he stated that only Delacroix and Rembrandt painted the figure of Christ effectively from a religious point of view.

Again, Vincent is responding to a letter with ten enclosed drawings he received from Bernard, but all such letters by Bernard are lost. Apparently Bernard had quoted lines from Baudelaire's *Flowers of Evil* that refer to a Rembrandt painting Baudelaire described as "a sad hospital filled full with murmurings." Vincent accuses Baudelaire (and Bernard) of failing to understand Rembrandt and Dutch art generally. My guess is that Vincent is objecting to Bernard (and Baudelaire) interpreting Rembrandt within their own rather mystical "symbolist" manner of seeking secret symbol-systems emerging from the artist's imagination rather than from engagement with the "real world." Further, I would guess that Vincent has some misgivings regarding Bernard's fixation on drawing scenes from brothels, evidenced in the drawings he sent to Vincent with his letter. Vincent will place over against both symbolism's imaginative mysticism and Bernard's rather "voyeuristic" approach to the brothel, the simplicity of family life and everyday scenes painted by the great Dutch artists. This leads Vincent to describe the Dutch artists in a manner that gets him tangled in contradictions. He wrote approvingly of the Dutch artists: "Those Dutchman had scarcely any imagination or fantasy, but great taste and the art of arrangement; they didn't paint Jesus Christs, the Good Lord and others" (Letter 649). But then Vincent realized he had entered a problem area, for Rembrandt's images of Christ were favorites of his: "Rembrandt though—indeed, but he's the *only one* (and there are relatively few biblical subjects in his oeuvre), he's the only one who, as an exception, did Christs, etc." Vincent then added of Rembrandt that "in his case they hardly resemble anything by other religious painters; it's metaphysical magic." He follows this with a description of Rembrandt painting himself as an old man, and adding "a supernatural angel with a Da Vinci smile."

By now, Vincent realizes that he has written himself into a corner, and attempts to explain the apparent inconsistency of his words to Bernard:

> I'm showing you a painter who dreams and who paints from the imagination, and I started off by claiming that the character of the Dutch is that they invent nothing, that they have neither imagination nor fantasy.

Am I illogical? No. *Rembrandt* invented nothing, and that
angel and that strange Christ; it's—that he knew them, *felt* them
there.

Vincent then goes on to refer to Delacroix's Christ, expressed through "an
unexpected lemon note" that gives the "ineffable strangeness and charm of
a star in a corner of the firmament."

The manner in which Vincent got himself into this tangle while trying
to oppose imaginative fantasy with Dutch everyday scenes in art, and his
rather unconvincing manner of trying to extricate himself, are significant.
How can he support the imagined images of Christs and angels of Rembrandt and Delacroix, yet oppose the symbolists' abandoning engagement
with the real world for a world of imagined symbols and secrets? In chapter
6, on symbolism, in my first book, *Van Gogh and God*, I contrast Vincent's
use of Zola's definition of art, "a work of art is a corner of nature seen
through a temperament" with the symbolist view espoused by Gauguin
and Bernard, "Art is an abstraction; extract it from nature while dreaming
before it."[2] Vincent wishes to affirm the world itself through his attending
to that which is nearest to him in everyday existence, but his attachment to
images of Christ by Rembrandt and Delacroix fly in the face of this devotion to the ordinary. He must therefore affirm: Rembrandt "knew" Christ
and the angel, he "*felt* them there."

Have we then experienced the moment when Vincent became aware
of the quandary he was in? Is his struggle over Christ and angel images
a very personal glimpse of "art as personal autobiography" in the life of
Vincent van Gogh? Where would he go from this tangle he has created as
his deep spirituality and its attachment to the life of Christ collides with his
devotion to the everyday world? Does an imitation of Christ call upon the
artist to seek the image of Christ through an experience of knowing and
feeling Christ's presence, and to paint that experience as Rembrandt did?
Or is the devoted artist-monk called upon to erase the image of Christ as an
act of devotion to the very art of Christ, the affirmation in the parables of
what was nearest in the real world to Christ himself: the sower, the harvest,
the fig tree? Is the struggle of Christ in Gethsemane to deal with the cup of
suffering the very struggle Vincent embodies in his search for an authentic
art for the future? Was Vincent's painting of Gethsemane a self-portrait of
his own struggle between devotion to Christ and his call to be an artist of
the here and now?

2. Edwards, *Van Gogh and God*, 130.

I believe it is only a year and many crises later that Vincent comes to some provisional resolution of this crucial problem regarding the relation of his personal spirituality to his practice of art. And it is in another letter to Bernard that he seeks to express his discovery and the direction it will take his art. But let us follow the months leading up to that letter of November 26, 1889, from the asylum of Saint Rémy to Bernard.

10

Yellow House to Asylum

Vincent's life during the months leading up to his letter to Bernard on November 26, 1889 includes some of his most intense periods of painting, worries over money, guilt at the burden Theo must bear, anxiety regarding the health of Gauguin in Brittany, hopes for an association of artists, and a series of health crises of his own.

A letter dated July 29, 1888 seeks to encourage Theo, who is seriously depressed and has written of the "emptiness" he feels. Vincent tells him that "you're more productive than me," that the more Theo as dealer helps artists, "the more you are an artist." Vincent affirms that they are both part of a "great revival of art that includes things so spiritual that a kind of melancholy remains with us" (Letter 650). In letters of late July and early August to Bernard, Vincent continues his argument that Dutch artists pursue "the great and simple thing, the painting of humanity." He affirms that Bernard was closest to Rembrandt when he painted his own grandmother, though Bernard's interests are apparently leading him to examine "the symbolic meaning that the Italians' abstract and mystical drawings may contain" (Letters 651, 655).

In mid-August, Vincent writes to Theo discussing a topic from the past that now becomes a lively hope, the possibility that they might establish in the South a center for an association of artists, "Living more or less like monks or hermits, with work as our ruling passion," joined together as the "Brethren of the Common Life" once did in the "Dutch heartlands" (Letter 660). But these artist-monks are seen by Vincent as devoted to Nature, the stars, and especially the southern sun. On August 18 he writes Theo: "And still to feel the stars and infinite, clearly up there. Then life is almost magical, after all. Ah, those who don't believe in the sun down here are truly blasphemous" (Letter 663). Similarly, to his youngest sister Wil, Vincent advises reading Whitman's poems on love, friendship, work, and the "starry firmament . . . that one could only call God and eternity, put back in place above this world" (Letter 670).

In early September, perhaps stimulated by conversations with the young Belgian painter, Eugene Boch, Vincent pens one of the most "spiritual" descriptions of his purpose in art to Theo. The "power to create," when addressing Theo, stands in for God or Christ:

> In life and in painting too, I can easily do without the dear Lord, but I can't, suffering as I do, do without something greater than myself, which is my life, the power to create. . . . And in a painting I'd like to say something consoling, like a piece of music. I'd like to paint men and women with that *je ne sais quoi* of the eternal, of which the halo used to be the symbol, and which we try to achieve through the radiance itself, through the vibrancy of our colorations. (Letter 673)

The same letter contains one of his most pointed descriptions of the sort of natural symbolism Vincent hoped to discover in his use of colors and elements of nature itself:

> I still have hopes of finding something there. To express the love of two lovers through a marriage of two complementary colours, their mixture and their contrasts, the mysterious vibrations of adjacent tones. To express the thought of a forehead through the radiance of a light tone on a dark background. To express hope through some star. The ardour of a living being through the rays of a setting sun. That's certainly not *trompe-l'oeil* realism, but isn't it something that really exists?

Through September, Vincent expressed his excitement in creating "an Artist's House" with money Theo provided. He worked "like a painting-locomotive," and waited impatiently to learn whether the ill Gauguin would come from Brittany to share the Yellow House and so establish the community of artists in a "studio of the South." In his excitement and surge of work, Vincent noted that he did a "lot of unforeseen things," and this might refer to the second of his paintings of Christ and the angel in the Garden of Olives. He confesses scraping off that second attempt in his letter of September 21, the following letter that expresses great interest in an article on Tolstoy, who is "searching for what will remain eternally true in the religion of Christ" (Letter 686). In a letter to Theo on September 29, Vincent again refers to religion, but seems almost apologetic about sharing such thoughts. Working on difficult paintings, he notes, is good for him, but "that doesn't stop me having a tremendous need for, shall I say the word—for religion—so I go outside at night to paint the stars." In the same letter, he wonders what a Benedictine priest Theo had met would say about the future of religion. Vincent goes on: "He'll probably say, still the same as the past. *Victor Hugo says, God is a lighthouse whose beam flashes on and off,* and so now, of course, we're passing through that darkness." Vincent then expresses the "wish" that:

> they could manage to prove something that would be calming to
> us, that would console us so that we'd cease to feel guilty or un-
> happy, and that just as we are we could proceed without getting
> lost in loneliness or nothingness, and without having at each step
> to fear or nervously calculate the harm which, without wishing to,
> we might cause others. (Letter 691)

It appears to me that the confessional element in this "wish" is summing up not only some of Vincent's own inner feelings, but may be seeking to include the sense of distress expressed in a lost letter by Theo. Perhaps in both cases we have reflections of the life and lessons the two brothers received in the Van Gogh parsonage years before, lessons that stirred up fears of failure and guilt at doing less than the family and its biblical injunctions required.

Letters in early October include revealing words by Gauguin to Vincent and words by Vincent to both Gauguin and Bernard that address differences in their approaches to painting. Gauguin describes the intent of his self-portrait sent to Vincent in terms of his eyes and nose appearing like "flowers in Persian carpets," which epitomize "an abstract and symbolic art" (Letter 692). Vincent's response of October 3 expresses his own approach, accompanied by a humble sense of failure: "I forget everything for the external beauty of things, *which I'm unable to render*" (Letter 695). Vincent rejects what must have been a sort of "symbolist manifesto" sent to him by Bernard. Vincent writes, "The idea of making a kind of freemasonry of painters doesn't please me hugely; I deeply despise rules" (Letter 696). Vincent follows on October 5 with another letter to Bernard, this one describing the Christ and angel in Gethsemane he destroyed. In answer to Bernard's urging Vincent to paint abstractions from the imagination, Vincent writes: "I have so much curiosity for what's possible and what really exists that I have so little desire or courage to search for the ideal, in so far as it could result from *my* abstract studies" (Letter 698). We have seen just a few glimpses of Vincent's life and work from late summer to fall 1888. Much was yet to happen before he was to receive photos of Bernard's paintings of Christ, including a "Christ in Gethsemane." At 5 in the morning of October 21, 1888, Gauguin arrived in Arles and spent sixty-three days at the Yellow House, painting, visiting cafés and brothels, discussing art and artists, and visiting a museum in Montpellier with Vincent. After very "electric" arguments, Vincent suffered what some speak of as "an acute mental breakdown" that included his cutting off a portion of his left ear and coming dangerously close to bleeding to death. Admitted to the hospital in Arles on December 24 of 1888, he returned to the Yellow House on January 7, 1889 and began painting again, as his self-portraits with bandaged ear reveal. On February 4 he had a second "mental breakdown" and returned to the hospital. He returned to the Yellow House again briefly, but a petition on March 19 signed by a number of neighbors asked he be locked up as dangerous, and he was placed in an isolation cell in the hospital. We have a letter from Vincent on May 2 to sister Wil, where he praises her for caring for a woman with cancer: "you're very brave, my sister, not to recoil before these Gethsemanes" (Letter 764). Perhaps his use of the word "Gethsemane" here suggests that he might be thinking of his own difficulties in such terms. His last letter from Arles, before being admitted to the asylum at Saint Rémy, was written on May 3, and in it he notes that he has pictures on his hospital wall, including pages of Japanese art and Delacroix's Pietà and Good Samaritan. He may still have been thinking wistfully of that lost hope for a community of artists in Arles. He writes Theo: "They have a lot of room here at the hospital, there'd be enough to make studios for thirty or so painters."

On May 8 Vincent was admitted to the asylum in Saint Rémy, not far from Arles, and Dr. Peyron wrote in the register that Van Gogh was "subject to attacks of epilepsy." By July 14 Vincent had another attack, repeated in December to January of 1890, and again between February and March. He painted some of his most famous works when he was able in the periods between attacks. In May, he expressed the wish to return to the North and visit Theo. Theo was now married and with a son born on January

31, named after Vincent. Discharged from the asylum, Vincent traveled by train to Paris to visit Theo, Johanna, and their son, and then moved to a rented attic room in the village of Auvers-sur-Oise outside Paris. There he was awaited by Dr. Gachet, a friend of artists. At Auvers Vincent would paint seventy major paintings in seventy days, including portraits of Dr. Gachet. Exhausted, fearing another attack, and disturbed by news of illness and business problems plaguing Theo, Vincent shot himself on July 27 while out painting. He died two days later in that attic room in Auvers, with Theo present to comfort him. Vincent was then buried in the village cemetery of Auvers, with Theo, Bernard, and several other artists present at the funeral.

I I

Crisis after Crisis

The month of November 1889 may hold answers to the puzzle of the creation and destruction of Van Gogh's Gethsemane paintings. During that month he would receive the sketch of a Gethsemane painting by Paul Gauguin. He would also receive a photograph of a painting of Gethsemane by his friend Emile Bernard. Vincent responded to both. But to arrive at that seventh month of his stay at the asylum in Saint Rémy, we will first set the scene, by examining Vincent's response to suffering a serious breakdown at the beginning of August, an attack that may have threatened his life and his art.

Vincent's early weeks at the asylum gave him hope that he would recover from the episodes that afflicted him and sent him to a sick-ward at the hospital in Arles, from his ear cutting to the petition that sent him to a hospital isolation cell. He felt himself recovering in the disciplined life of the asylum. He painted in the institution's garden and beyond, irises, lilacs, the wheatfield outside his barred window, olive orchards close to the asylum wall, cypresses, and his famous *Starry Night*.

But just past the middle of July, a serious crisis occurred during which it is reported that he poisoned himself and harmed his throat with paint and brush. He was left dizzy and confused for days, and became "absolutely distraught" as he reported to Theo (Letter 797). For almost two months he would not go "out in the open air," feeling a "deep sadness" and "fear of the other patients" (Letters 798, 801). His response was to seek to cure himself, or at least drive away the fears and nightmares, by the labor of painting. On September 6 he wrote Theo, "I'm working non-stop in my room," seeking to drive "abnormal thoughts away." The scene from his barred window over a walled wheatfield gave him some consoling access to nature, and he struggled to complete the painting of a reaper in the wheatfield he had begun just before his attack.

The age-old view that God has given us two books, the Bible and the Book of Nature, became a theme in his work, including the painting of the reaper. He wrote Theo:

> I then saw in this reaper—a vague figure struggling like a devil in the full heat of the day to reach the end of his toil—I then saw the image of death in it, in this sense that humanity would be the wheat being reaped. . . . But in this death nothing sad, it takes place in broad daylight with a sun that floods everything with the light of fine gold. (Letter 800)

Later in that same letter he returns to this theme and its symbolism that moves him deeply: "—it's an image of death as the great book of nature speaks to us about it."

The power that such a scene of a human laboring in nature had for him is amplified when he continues to Theo, who with wife Johanna, is awaiting the birth of a child:

> Ah well, do you know what I hope for once I set myself to having some hope, it's that the family will be for you what nature is for me, the mounds of earth, the grass, the yellow wheat, the peasant. That's to say that you will find in your love for people the wherewithal *not only to work* but the wherewithal to console you and restore you when you need it. (Letter 800)

Vincent's description of the scene through his bars, the peasant with a sickle bent over the ripe wheat in the golden sunshine, might well bring to mind that scene beside the monastery ruins of Montmajour, that shower of gold he saw that may have been seen by him as a yellow angel comforting Jesus in agony at Gethsemane. In his letter to Theo, the Book of Nature's spiritual message of comfort may be as close as he wished to approach the consoling angel with Christ in that other book, the Bible. The natural symbolism of ripened wheat and the labor of a peasant in its midst seem to lose nothing of the power a biblical scene may have offered, and certainly calls to mind the symbols employed by that "greatest of artists" in his parables of sowing and reaping. If Vincent is not writing of Christ to Theo, he is doing in paint what Christ himself was doing in words. Vincent was painting parables that linked God's two great books.

The peasant's labor just outside his window must have resonated with Vincent's own passion to work as a pathway toward a cure, or at least as a comfort in dizzying illness. In this same letter he repeats again that "if there is a remedy it is to work passionately," and he can describe his labor of painting as "the best lightning conductor for the illness" (Letter 800).

The very next letter to Theo, on September 10, reveals the artist's sense that things are being revealed to him through his own struggle with illness and passion for healing work. He writes Theo that "I'm finding things that I've sought in vain for years" (Letter 801). His crises, he goes on to say, "tend to take an absurd religious turn" there in the old monastery cloisters of the asylum, but he also notes that "in the very suffering religious thoughts sometimes console me a great deal" (Letter 801). On that subject, he reports the accident during his illness that spoiled his Delacroix lithograph of the Pietà. He reports that he immediately worked to replace the damaged sheet with his own painting of it. The Christ image must certainly have been part of his religious consolation in illness, though he restricts his comments to Theo to the act of restoration through his art.

Thoughts of Delacroix led Vincent to the word "Gethsemane" and a revealing observation on the importance of "place" in creating a scene from Christ's life. The "allure" of Delacroix's paintings, he writes, occurs:

> Because E. Delacroix, when he does a Gethsemane, went to see on the spot beforehand what an olive grove was like, and the same for the sea whipped up by a hard mistral, and because he must have said to himself, these people whom history talks about, doges of Venice, crusaders, apostles, holy women, were of the same type and lived in a manner analogous to those of their present-day descendants. (Letter 801)

Vincent's acute sense of the importance of "place," of knowing both the natural and cultural context of what one is painting, is expressed forcefully here. Delacroix's travels to the Mediterranean had allowed him to study the look of an olive grove for his *The Agony in the Garden* and a tempest at sea for his *Christ Asleep during the Tempest*. Such visual understanding in regard to Christ in Palestine found support in Vincent's favorite *Life of Christ* by Renan, written in large part as Renan's response to his living among those descendants of Jesus' people and his hiking Jesus' path along the Sea of Galilee and on the Mount of Olives. Vincent's reference to Delacroix doing a "Gethsemane" is interesting in that olive trees play little role in the painting. Its creative element would seem to be the focus on the image of Jesus visited by three young and beautiful female angels who weep at the thought of his coming passion.

Were Vincent's experiences of Mediterranean sun and sea and olive trees enough to qualify him to paint a Jesus in Gethsemane? Perhaps Vincent posed this question to himself when he painted and repainted, destroyed and destroyed again his Gethsemane works. Was the analogy of Arles' peasant to Palestinian peasant, Montmajour olive grove to Mount of Olives strong enough to warrant his attempt at a biblical painting? Could he find a "model" for Jesus and the angel in Arles, or must one "feel" such presences as did Rembrandt?

But now, in the asylum, there was another issue. Did Vincent any longer have the strength, particularly the emotional strength, to attempt such works? He puzzles over this to Theo, but again without focusing overmuch on the religious content of the question:

> So I must tell you it, and you can see it in the Berceuse, however failed and weak that attempt may be. Had I the strength to continue, I'd have done portraits of saints and holy women from life, and who would have appeared to be from another century and they would be citizens of the present day, and yet would have something in common with very primitive Christians.
>
> The emotion that that causes are too strong though, I wouldn't survive it—but later, later, I don't say that I won't mount a fresh attack. (Letter 801)

Vincent goes on to reflect on advice Theo must have emphasized in recent letters:

> You're right a thousand times over—one mustn't think about all that—one must do—even if it's studies of cabbages and salad to calm oneself down, and after being calmed then—what one is capable of. (Letter 801)

And so Vincent, at this juncture in his life, turned to "repetitions" of former works of his own and "interpretations" in color of Millet's *The Labours of the Fields* and similar prints.

What does this tell us of Vincent and the paintings he would have attempted if he were well? Did he hope to find citizens of Arles who could serve as models for Christ and the early Christians? Would his use of Augustine Roulin and Marie Ginoux as the sisters of Lazarus in his painting of a portion of that Rembrandt etching give us a sense of his intent? Does his observation that he "wouldn't survive" such labor suggest the dizziness of ecstatic visions on Montmajour or in parable-like fields with sowers and reapers? Is the very challenge he presented to himself in painting a Gethsemane an incarnation of his very struggle to discern the nature of the cup facing him in his choice of subject for his canvases? Was the Gethsemane painting spiritual autobiography that required both creation and destruction?

Perhaps Vincent's choice of the asylum and his willingness to work at "studies of cabbages" was for the sake of brother Theo who had already sacrificed so much for him. Theo was often ill, almost always depressed and burdened, and now was a concerned father-to-be, who also happened to avoid religious topics. But even if this is so, Vincent's energies and vision often took him beyond cabbages. He copied Delacroix's *Pietà*. From his barred window he painted a reaper as symbol of death in a parable-like wheatfield. He painted a whole series of canvases devoted to the very setting of the Gethsemane scene, actual olive orchards. To these he would add a *Garden of the Asylum* with a broken tree and dying rose as symbolic of Gethsemane, as we will now hear him explain in a letter to Bernard.

12

Refusing Medieval Tapestries

The month of November 1889 is a critical one in our search for Vincent's views regarding his ghost paintings and the possibility of doing images from the life of Christ as a legitimate part of the art of his time. Letters during that month brought word and images to Vincent of two paintings of Christ in Gethsemane, both by his closest artist friends, Gauguin and Bernard. A letter to Vincent from Gauguin on November 13 described "a thing I haven't sent and which would suit you, I think," a "Christ in the Garden of Olives" which "isn't destined to be understood." Gauguin sketched an image of this painting in color in his letter (Letter 817). Then on November 16 Theo wrote that he had visited Bernard's studio and described for Vincent one of the paintings he had seen there:

> He's also done a Christ in the Garden of Olives. A red-headed,
> violet Christ with a yellow angel. It's very difficult to understand,
> and the search for style often lends something ridiculous to his
> figures, but perhaps something good will come of it. (Letter 819)

So November 1889 became a very special month with two Geth-semanes by two admired artists coming to the attention of Vincent van Gogh. By November 26 Vincent had received and responded to a now-lost letter from Bernard with photographs of that very "Christ in the Garden of Olives" mentioned by Theo. The collection of photos contained at least three other Bernard paintings on the life of Christ. And so in this one

month, his seventh at the asylum, Vincent clearly saw that his two closest artist friends had been working at scenes from the life of Christ over
a year after he had painted and destroyed his two attempts at Christ and
the angel in Gethsemane. Within a month after Vincent responded to the
images sent by Gauguin and Bernard, he would have another attack. Then
in February-March he would have a further attack. By May he would decide it was best to leave the asylum and return to the north. He enjoyed a
visit to Theo, Johanna, and their new child Vincent, his godchild, in Paris.
Within days he would settle some miles from Paris in the little village of
Auvers-sur-Oise where a Dr. Gachet had promised Theo he would watch
over brother Vincent's health.

How Vincent responded to the Christ images painted by Bernard and
Gauguin adds critical material to the clues we found in his earlier letters
from Arles and from his first months at the Asylum. His pointed responses
to Bernard's photographs of paintings *Annunciation*, an *Adoration of the
Shepherds*, *Christ in the Garden of Olives*, and *Christ Carrying his Cross* are
both revealing and puzzling. Though Vincent begins by thanking Bernard
for the photos of the paintings, he is soon aiming some of his most passionate rhetoric against Bernard's biblical images. After praising a Bernard
painting of "nothing but three trees" that Gauguin had described for him,
Vincent writes:

> And when I compare that with that nightmare of a Christ in the
> Garden of Olives, well, it makes me feel sad, and I herewith ask
> you again, crying out loud and giving you a piece of my mind with
> all the power of my lungs, to please become a little more yourself
> again. (Letter 822)

Just a week before receiving and criticizing Bernard's photographs,
Vincent had written Theo his concerns after receiving the sketch of
Gauguin's *Christ in Gethsemane*. He wrote Theo on November 19, 1889:

> And I'm not an admirer of Gauguin's *Christ in the Garden of Olives*
> for example, a croquis of which he sent me. Then as for Bernard's,
> he promises me a photograph of it. I don't know, but I fear that his
> biblical compositions will make me wish for something else. . . .
> Now he therefore avoids conceiving the least idea of the possible
> and of the reality of things, and that isn't the way to synthesize.
> No, never have I got involved in their biblical interpretations. I
> said that Rembrandt and Delacroix had done this admirably, that
> I liked that even better than the primitives, but then stop. I don't

want to begin on that chapter again. If I remain here I wouldn't try
to paint a Christ in the Garden of Olives, but in fact the olive picking as it's still seen today, and then giving the correct proportions
of the human figure in it, that would perhaps make people think
of it all the same. Before I've done more serious studies than I have
up to now I don't have the right to get involved in this. (Letter 820)

Does Vincent mean that the setting of an olive orchard with human figures
in the scene should bring Gethsemane to the viewer's mind? Does he mean
he will not return to painting a Christ image, or does he mean he might
return to the theme after a good bit more study and maturity as an artist?
Perhaps he is simply writing that he does not want to get involved in arguments regarding the biblical paintings of Bernard and Gauguin until he has
given the entire subject more thought.

Vincent's intent in his letter to Theo (Letter 820) becomes more focused when he goes on in his letter to Bernard (Letter 822), criticizing other
Bernard paintings of Christ: "The Christ carrying his Cross is atrocious.
Are the splashes of color in it harmonious? But I won't let you off the hook
for a COMMONPLACE—commonplace, you hear—in the composition."
Is it that Vincent finds no creative engagement in Bernard's view of the
scene? Is that what he means by "commonplace?" Is it that Bernard simply
reproduces images from the history of religious art? Is that why Vincent
destroyed his own Gethsemane paintings? Of Bernard's *The Adoration of
the Shepherds* Vincent criticizes the unnaturalness of the scene:

It's too great an impossibility to imagine a birth like that, on the
very road, the mother who starts praying instead of giving suck,
the fat ecclesiastical bigwigs, kneeling as if in an epileptic fit. God
knows how or why they're there, but I myself don't find it healthy.
(Letter 822)

Perhaps it is the "artificiality" of the mother's praying when she should be
at motherly nurturing, and the kneeling "ecclesiastical bigwigs" may call
to Vincent's mind the officious Board of Evangelism that rejected his sac-
rificial service to miners or the refusal of his father to read Zola or allow
the new French literature into the Van Gogh parsonage. Vincent goes on
to place over-against Bernard's "unnatural" painting of the birth of Christ
a canvas he remembers by the peasant-artist Millet, *Birth of the Calf*. He
cleverly works much of his own critique of the Bernard painting into his
description of the Millet:

Because I adore the true, the possible, were I ever capable of spiritual fervor; so I bow before that study, so powerful that it makes you tremble, by père Millet—peasants carrying to the farmhouse a calf born in the fields. Now, my friend—people have felt that from France to America. After that would you go back to renewing medieval tapestries for us?

It is fascinating that Vincent here actually discerns the direction Bernard's art was to take. Once at the forefront of a post-Impressionist movement, Bernard returned to a conservative Catholic tradition and, in spite of his admiration for Vincent, spent much of the rest of his life creating church decorations, traditional murals of crucifixion scenes and saints. Bernard, did, in fact, quite purposefully return to "medieval tapestries."

But let us penetrate the meaning of Vincent's choice of a painting by the peasant-artist, Jean-Francois Millet, as a spiritual work worthy of adoration. The painting, largely in earth colors, pictures a farmer and his field-hand carrying between them a pallet with a newborn calf resting on a bed of hay, while the mother cow walks alongside, attended by the farmer's wife. The farmhouse is in sight, and excited children await the arrival of that calf born in the fields, likely soon to be their new housemate. One might compare the scene with Vincent's much earlier description of the birth of Sien's child in that charity ward: "And even if it was a hospital where she lay and I sat with her, it's always that eternal poetry of Christmas night with the baby in the manger" (Letter 245). A new life, whether human, animal, or sprouting wheat, is an everyday miracle that is both reality and symbol. Vincent put it simply: "All reality is also symbolic at the same time" (Letter 533). A newborn calf and our caring for it, provides an image charged with significance accessible to all. It speaks of the radical incarnation of divine presence, the something on high and the something deep within that brings an ecstatic awakening to those with eyes to see. It encourages our devotion to what is nearest, rather than tempting us to dream of medieval tapestries in our search for the sacred.

As I read Vincent's words regarding the Millet painting of the newborn calf as his prime example of truly "religious" art, I recalled an experience Vincent had recounted to Theo in 1882 from The Hague. Writing of a painting of the birth of Christ he had seen in a studio and his sense that its "expression" was not right, he immediately turned the subject to the birth of a calf:

I saw it once in real life, not the birth of the baby Jesus, mind you, but the birth of a calf. And I still know exactly what its expression was like. There was a girl there, at night in that stable—in the Borinage—a brown peasant face with a white night-cap among other things, she had tears in her eyes of compassion for the poor cow when the animal went into labour and was having great difficulty. It was pure, holy, wonderfully beautiful like a Correggio, like a Millet, like an Israels. Oh, Theo, why don't you let it all go hang and become a painter? (Letter 211)

My own guess is that Vincent's sense of religious symbolism, often linked through an association of vivid memories, connected the birth of that calf in the Borinage, the compassion of the child, Luke's Christmas story set at a manger, and the children in Millet's painting waiting to greet the tired Mother cow and her newborn calf. His very impractical suggestion that Theo become a painter arose from his own sense of the wonder of rendering such moments in paint.

In his letter to Bernard, Vincent not only provides a description of this Millet work as an alternative to Bernard's paintings from the life of Christ, but goes on to describe two of his own recent canvases as illustrations of symbolic layers of meaning residing in the reality of the things closest to us. One painting, done in the asylum park, pictures a tree broken by lightning beside the last rose on a withered bush. Vincent explains that the scene offers the viewer a "sensation of anguish" called "noir-rouge" or more likely "voir-rouge," "to see-red," a term used for some of the forms of mental anguish encountered at the asylum. A contrasting canvas pictures the "sun rising over a field of young wheat," which gives the sense of "calmness, a great peace." Vincent explains them to Bernard:

I'm speaking to you of these two canvases . . . to remind you that in order to give an impression of anxiety, you can try to do it without heading straight for the historic Garden of Gethsemane; in order to offer a consoling and gentle subject it isn't necessary to depict the figures from the Sermon on the Mount—(Letter 822)

Vincent's intent in these examples from Millet and his own paintings raises serious questions. Does he believe that the response of the viewer to the newborn calf, the broken tree, and the sun over young wheat will actually bring the nativity of Christ, Gethsemane, and the Sermon on the Mount to the viewer's mind? Or is there an equivalent feeling he expects in the response one has to these scenes and the response one might expect from the events in the story of Christ? Is there hidden in the scenes of the here and now painted by the sensitive artist some pathway that leads toward the revelation made available in the biblical events? Is Vincent using the very transformative technique Jesus used in his parables of sowers, reapers, and fig trees to open the feelings of humans to these deeper responses to the world? If so, Vincent is imitating Christ not through the scenes of Christ's life but through the manner of Christ's observing and sharing his understanding of what is closest. The artist, like Christ, can use the present world familiar to his listeners to open symbolic pathways of feeling and so of meaning. Might such images of the here and now actually serve as symbols of the deeper meaning of birth, death, and compassion? For some, might they even call to mind the life drama of Christ in his birth among the poor, his sermon on love, comfort, and caring, and his agony of choosing the difficult path of service even to the point of personal sacrifice? I think Vincent would have allowed for all these possibilities.

But we have a further illustration of Vincent's sense of the revelatory power of images taken from the here and now to summon deep religious feelings. Perhaps Vincent finally provides a "model" for the image of Christ through a healer and nurturer on the contemporary scene. In his dealings with Paul Gauguin, Vincent often takes the stance of a pupil honoring a seasoned teacher. Gauguin's authority, though certainly not beyond reproach in Vincent's mind, nevertheless seems to lead Vincent to couch his criticism of Gauguin's biblical scenes more obliquely. Further, there is some complexity in Gauguin's biblical paintings that is absent from those of Bernard. Contemporary figures, for example, were included by Gauguin along with biblical characters in his *Vision after the Sermon: Jacob Wrestling with the Angel*. Gauguin's Gethsemane painting may also contain a complexity, as the image of Christ could easily be viewed as a self-portrait of Gauguin himself. Nevertheless, Vincent, in the draft of a letter he never got to send, seems to suggest to Gauguin that rather than attempting a painting of Christ in Gethsemane one might find the same "expression" on the face of a neighbor, in this case Vincent's own melancholy physician-friend in the village of Auvers:

> Now I have a portrait of Dr. Gachet with the deeply sad expression of our time. *If you like*, something like what you were saying about your Christ in the Garden of Olives, not destined to be understood. (RM23)

Vincent's memory for images may well have led him to pose Dr. Gachet in the very same "melancholic" posture as an image of Christ sometimes attributed to Albrecht Durer. In the Durer image Christ holds hyssop, the plant associated with the crucifixion, in the exact manner Gachet, in one version of the Auvers portrait, holds the foxglove plant used in medicine. Here, perhaps, in his physician friend, Vincent has in fact found a "model" for Christ and painted the one original Christ image he was willing to leave for posterity. Certainly Vincent knew Christ's claim that he came "not to heal the well but the sick," and Vincent was one of the sick Dr. Gachet offered to heal. What could be closer to Vincent's experience of a healer than the melancholy doctor who welcomed him into his home, family, and garden, and urged him to continue painting.

Returning to Vincent's argument in the letter to Bernard, we see Vincent returning to the hold present reality had on him, his responsibility for the events of his own time:

> Ah—it is—no doubt—wise, right, to be moved by the Bible, but modern reality has such a hold over us that even when trying abstractly to reconstruct ancient times in our thoughts—just at that very moment the petty events of our lives tear us away from these meditations and our own adventures throw us forcibly into personal sensations: joy, boredom, suffering, anger or smiling. (Letter 822)

Abstract dreams of images from the past, illustrations of texts and interpretations provided by others and solidified by authorities through institutional traditions, were not Vincent's way in either art or spirituality. Academic schools of art with their dogmas, and institutional religion with its self-righteous certainties, were temptations Vincent refused. He struggled with the reality nearest to him. If the depth of spiritual meaning were not available in the peasant hut, the newborn calf, and the field of wheat, then it would not be worthy of the artist's search and struggle. As Jesus had described in one of his parables, the "hidden treasure" is buried right in the field you plow. Vincent put the truth very simply to sister Wil: "one has to do what lies to hand" (Letter 626). Likewise, to Theo, he had written the same advice: "let's do the possible, what is right in front of us" (Letter 621).

The German poet Rainer Maria Rilke marveled at the effectiveness of that truth after seeing in Paris an "astonishing" portfolio of prints of Vincent's work in 1907. Rilke wrote to his wife back in Germany:

I believe I do feel what van Gogh must have felt at a certain juncture, and it is a strong and great feeling: that everything is yet to
be done: everything. But this devotion to what is nearest, this is
something I can't do as yet, or only in my best moments, while it is
at one's worst moments that one really needs it.[1]

Rilke recognized the difficulty of achieving what he identified as
unique in Vincent's art, a "devotion to what is nearest." Further, he linked
this devotion to the "great feeling ...that everything is yet to be done."
New meaning is located in whatever is closest, a freshness is brought to
each scene, event, and the task of engaging it. Never would one be without
subjects or opportunities in a constant renewal of one's art. So Vincent,
while living at the parsonage in the Village of Nuenen, attended to its most
ordinary and forgotten citizens and sites, the peasants and weavers in their
thatched cottages. Three years later, living in the Ginoux lodging house in
Arles, Vincent simply walked downstairs to the Night Café and painted
those left behind when all others had returned to their homes. That which
was nearest for the artist was the forgotten underside of society, always present but seldom noticed. Vincent painted those marginalized people from
the heart, and painted them as one living among them. Indoors or out, Vincent set himself to paint the most ordinary: peasant, postman, housewife,
empty chair, worn shoes, dusty thistle, empty path, or windblown wheat.

For a pilgrim artist, viewed by many as a "madman and criminal,"
painting what was nearest was painting the dispossessed, the poor. The
mission of the artist who had once hoped to "preach the gospel to the
poor" was to show the world that there was heart and soul in discarded or
forgotten persons and places. These "showings" were a healing ministry in
themselves. First, they intended to awaken "civilized" society to persons
and places it refused to see, hopefully awakening some to a new sense of
reality and responsibility in the confused world beset by the forces of industrialization, urbanization, exploitation, and class conflict.

Second, dignity was bestowed upon the lowliest sufferers through an
honest portrayal of their plight and their hopes by one living among them
with his own plight and hopes. Seeing ordinary people as worthy of attention, and painting them at their daily tasks by one living among them was
a healing act. Similarly, the hidden corners of a garden, a simple bedroom,
ivy climbing a tree, were painted and so rescued from the obscurity left to

1. Rilke, *Letters on Cézanne*, 22–23.

them by a society willing to notice only the impressive and traditionally beautiful aspects of nature.

Vincent had himself experienced the Gethsemane of agonizing struggle over the direction of his art. He had seen himself as well as Christ in need of a comforting angel in the Garden of Olives. Perhaps Theo was that angel for Vincent. Perhaps the comforting angel had many transformations: the olive trees, the cypresses, the germinating wheat, the sun and the rainstorm, a postal worker, a child. Vincent may have had to paint Gethsemane to realize the meaning of a lifetime struggle for a cause, and he may have had to destroy the Gethsemane scene because the cause to which he was called was a devotion to what was nearest him in the world of the dispossessed and forgotten. Perhaps he found that though he needed on his wall the images of Christ as "felt" by Rembrandt and Delacroix, his own "feelings" as laboring artist were better engaged by the sufferings and needs, the storms and growth he experienced in his own time and place. He may well have learned in his Gethsemane paintings that his personal, hidden spiritual needs responding to the old biblical symbols were one thing, but his calling to paint the meanings hidden in his own day was another.

Vincent's appreciation for the Bible as "light in the darkness," yet his turning toward the duty to our own time and place was not a new thought. A letter he wrote to his youngest sister Wil in late October 1887, one of his few letters from Paris, takes us back to his thoughts before Arles, before his Gethsemane paintings, and before his months at the asylum. Recommending contemporary authors to Wil, who wanted to become a writer, he advised:

> The work of the French naturalists Zola, Flaubert, Guy de Maupassant, De Goncourt, Richepin, Daudet, Huysmans is magnificent and one can scarcely be said to belong to one's time if one isn't familiar with them. (Letter 574)

He goes on to pose a question that likely was asked in Wil's own lost letter to him: "Is the Bible enough for us? Nowadays I believe Jesus himself would again say to those who just sit melancholy, *it is not here, it is risen. Why seek ye the living among the dead?*" Vincent goes on to call for current speaking and writing that is "as great and as good as the original," that is as capable as was the Bible "of overturning the whole old society as in the past." He notes that his own reading of the Bible has given him "a certain peace that there have been such lofty ideas in the past." It is this that leads him to honor the Bible not by attaching himself to it, but by turning with that same passion to the creative works and puzzling issues of meaning in his own time and task:

> But precisely because I think the old is good, I find the new all the more so. All the more so because we can take action ourselves in our own age, and both the past and the future affect us only indirectly.

But writing as an artist to his youngest sister who was considering becoming an artist, Vincent avoids making of art some privileged, high-priestly calling, as some were doing in his day, Bernard included. He questions whether "religion or law or art" should be considered "so sacred?" He suggests to Wil that "people who do nothing other than fall in love are perhaps more serious and holier than those who sacrifice their love and their heart to an idea." Vincent may well be indicating that even a work of art may be given up for the enrichment of the life of ordinary people, and perhaps one should be willing to sacrifice art itself if such sacrifice nurtures and deepens the blossoming of life amid the daily challenges and sorrows of one's own time.

13

The Secret Life of Artistic Creation

As we began this quest for Van Gogh's "ghost paintings," I expressed the following view of their importance:

> I believe that the two unique paintings Vincent created and destroyed are at least as important to understanding the artist and his work as are the two thousand or more paintings and drawings that do exist. I believe that devoting attention to the ghost paintings will reveal an illuminating new dimension of Vincent's struggle to discover the spiritual dimension of art for the culture of his day and ours.

As we approach the end of our quest, allow me to defend those assertions and invite you to consider their merits.

I believe my focus on Vincent twice painting and destroying an original work of a sort he had never attempted before and never attempted again, at the very height of his painting career, cries out for careful attention. Our quest has sought to test the thesis that works destroyed by an artist, though never seen by us, may nevertheless be crucial to understanding the total intent of his life and work. Are we so prejudiced in favor of what we can see and possess that we largely ignore what is obviously significant to the artist yet purposely hidden from us? Shouldn't the mystery of a work that is purposely returned to the secret life of the artist's process attract us all the more poignantly and powerfully?

Let me give just a few examples of what I consider to be our failure to take serious notice and attempt thoughtful evaluation of such works, specifically the ghost paintings. The great Van Gogh scholar, Jan Hulsker, in the five hundred pages of his *The Complete Van Gogh: Paintings, Drawing, Sketches* takes no notice of those two paintings. He includes scores of marginal works that do exist, but passes over those two large paintings described with some care by the artist. Do such works forfeit their status within the artist's creative process because the artist twice decided to scrape them off yet chose to confess their creation to others? In his *Vincent and Theo Van Gogh: A Dual Biography*, a work of some 470 pages, Hulsker does direct one paragraph to the destroyed paintings, but only notes that if we did have them, it "would have shown that at this moment he was no less progressive than his two colleagues in Pont-Aven."[1] Isn't it likely it is the absence of these paintings that leads Hulsker to pass them off as simply "progressive"? Further, hasn't Hulsker gotten their meaning for Vincent and their relationship to the work of Gauguin and Bernard wrong? Vincent's destruction of his first Gethsemane painting was reported to Theo on July 8 or 9 of 1888, and it was October 5 of 1888 that he confessed destroying such a work to Bernard. But it was not until November of the following year, 1889, that Vincent received Bernard's photos of his paintings from the life of Christ and Gauguin's sketch of his *Christ in the Garden*. Vincent's *Gethsemane* was hardly an attempt to keep up with his friends so far as theme was concerned, as his work pre-dated theirs by almost a year. Further, his criticism of their Gethsemane scenes hardly viewed them as "progressive" as we detailed in the chapter "Refusing Medieval Tapestries." If by "progressive," Hulsker is thinking of the color descriptions, there are dozens of existing works by Vincent that would be better examples of his "progressive" work with color. Vincent destroyed his Gethsemane works in part not because they were "progressive," but because he felt they might be "regressive."

Another Van Gogh expert, Cornelia Homburg, does struggle creatively with the question of Vincent's approach to religious art, and mentions the destroyed Gethsemane paintings in both her *The Treasures of Vincent Van Gogh* (2007) and her earlier *The Copy Turns Original: Vincent van Gogh and a New Approach to Traditional Art Practice* (1996). But she seems to come close to forgetting or dismissing the destroyed Gethsemane paintings when

1. Hulsker, *Vincent and Theo Van Gogh*, 284.

she sums up Vincent's religious works. In her *The Copy Turns Original*, she writes:

> Van Gogh's critical opinion of religion was mirrored in his artistic work. He executed no compositions with religious subject-matter apart from his copies after Rembrandt and Delacroix in Saint Rémy. He might portray a church or an old churchyard as motifs that were part of his surroundings, but he did not depict a biblical scene.[2]

Certainly Homburg knew of the Gethsemane paintings, but her mind seems to have played a trick that may often be associated with works we cannot view. We simply "forget" that we know such works were part of the artist's creative process.

Finally, let me give one more example of a work on Van Gogh that dismisses Vincent's two paintings of Christ in Gethsemane in spite of the author's intent to focus on "the importance of his early Christian beliefs in shaping his artistic vision." In her volume *At Eternity's Gate: The Spiritual Vision of Vincent van Gogh*, Kathleen Powers Erickson sums up Vincent's Christian themes in art this way:

> An artist who painted more than thirty representations of sowers, as well as the overtly religious subjects of the raising of Lazarus, the Good Samaritan, and the Pietà, in which he depicted the face of Christ with the features of his own face, cannot be understood in terms of an absolute rejection of religion or Christianity.

This focus on Vincent's three "copied" paintings as the sum-total of his biblical subjects occurs later in her work: "During the St. Rémy period, van Gogh painted his first renditions of overtly Christian and biblical subjects: *The Pietà* (1889), *The Raising of Lazarus* (1890), and *The Good Samaritan* (1890)."[3]

Of course Erickson's general assertion of the influence of Christianity in Vincent's art is true, but it is especially revealing that in making her case she omits the only two original paintings in which he chose for himself a scene from the life of Christ, the two Gethsemane paintings. She concentrates on such symbolic themes as the sower and his copies of the works of others, specifically Rembrandt and Delacroix. This is all the more revealing in that she does know of his Gethsemane paintings and can refer

2. Homberg, *The Copy Turns Original*, 65.
3. Ibid.

to Vincent's own words regarding those works. She explains that he "was reluctant to paint a realistic representation of Christ because he felt Christ was too important a figure to paint without proper models, so adopted a symbolic vocabulary."[4] Erickson's erasure of the Gethsemane paintings from serious consideration simply reflects the assumptions of many critics in dismissing those works. The creative process of the artist, both original creation and original erasure, are not given their vital place in the struggle to find a personal pathway in art. That Vincent's choice of one spiritual route as artist over another led him to scrape off a scene in which Christ was agonizing over a similar life and death decision adds a poignant irony to the situation.

Another point of irony might well call into question how seriously we are to take Vincent's own excuse for the erasure of the Gethsemane paintings. We already noted that his words "I tell myself" that introduce his reasoning that "it's wrong to do figures of that importance without a model" (Letter 637) signal his own uncertainty regarding the legitimacy of his excuse for not allowing a painting of Christ to stand. Add to that the view Erickson shares with many critics that Vincent painted himself into the Christ figure in the Pietà. If he could use himself as a model in his copy of Delacroix's *Pietà*, in what sense was he without a model? Further, several images of Christ, including the images by Delacroix and Rembrandt had been hanging on his wall. Did he not use those images as models? I return then to my earlier view that Vincent's mind was struggling with complex feelings regarding the painting of Christ, as discussed in chapter 8, "Rembrandt's Christ and Vincent's Quandary." Rembrandt "felt" the presence of Christ and angels and could therefore legitimately paint them. Vincent's experience on Montmajour with its monastery ruins and its olive trees led him to test the possibility that he too might in the act of painting "feel" the presence of the Christ and an angel comforting and guiding his direction in art. His decision to erase his attempt, if I am correct, was either a recognition that Rembrandt's "feeling" was not available to him, or a decision that he had best keep the comforting presence of Christ secret, just as Jesus had preached that one's praying be done not like "the hypocrites" but secretly in one's closet (Matthew 6:5). Vincent's own experience with Christian hypocrites perhaps made it impossible for him to display his own paintings of Christ "on the street corners to be seen by men." One could live out of the hidden treasure of a personal Christ-mysticism and

4. Ibid., 99.

yet paint not Gethsemane, but the presence of the spirit in what was closest at hand. Vincent, perhaps, felt that he was called to paint what he saw
among the poor, but he also felt the presence of a secret life of the spirit
with its own agonizing search and hope for comfort. Perhaps we must take
account of two powerful facets to Vincent's pilgrimage. Vincent was called
to paint the spirit hidden in the ordinary, yet he longed for the comfort
of the Christ and angel whose images were provided by Rembrandt and
Delacroix. The images that sustained his own spiritual life must be hidden
in his secret life in order that those images not blind humanity to Christ in
the neighbor and in the Book of Nature. The agonizing necessity of scraping off the Gethsemane scene was incarnate in his very choice of the agony
of Jesus at that moment in the garden: "Yes, for me the drama of a storm in
nature, the drama of sorrow in life, is the best. A 'paradou' is beautiful, but
Gethsemane is more beautiful still" (Letter 381). Vincent lived and painted
with the sinners outside the Garden of Eden. He was a visual biographer
of humanity and nature outside Paradise. His calling required him to live
the life of another garden, Gethsemane, while hiding its image in his heart.

14

Empty Shoes on Empty Paths

It was over thirty years ago that I entered the new Van Gogh Museum in Amsterdam and stood in silence before Vincent's Paris painting *A Pair of Old Shoes*. I knew that this was the very painting that stopped Martin Heidegger in his tracks before I was born. Heidegger, in his lecture "The Origin of the Work of Art," wrote of that painting he had come upon in a gallery in Germany: From Van Gogh's painting we cannot even tell where these shoes stand. There is nothing surrounding this pair of peasant shoes in or to which they might belong—only an unidentified space.[1] Heidegger can be forgiven for taking a pair of urban work-shoes for the foot-wear of a peasant. His focus on our inability "to tell where these shoes stand" is especially interesting. That is exactly the case with Mu-ch'i's six persimmons, which seem to emerge from "nothingness" and float before the viewer in space. Later in his lecture, Heidegger tells us this about that painting of shoes:

> Thus art is the creative preserving of truth in the work. *Art then is the becoming and happening of truth.* Does truth, then, arise out of nothing? It does indeed if by nothing is meant the mere not of beings.[2]

1. Heidegger, "The Origin of the Work of Art," 163.
2. Ibid., 183.

We might say that the power of negation, presence hidden in absence, is here demonstrated as crossing cultural divides and meeting in the work of Mu-ch'i and Van Gogh.

After seeing Vincent's painting of empty shoes and musing on the essays of Heidegger, I drove from Holland through Belgium and then followed a narrow country road into France in search of the village of Auvers-sur-Oise where Vincent had spent his last seventy days, where he had painted his *Wheatfield with Crows* and had shot himself, and then later died in the attic room of a café. After stopping at more than one country store and asking directions, I finally arrived at Auvers, and entered the little café on the main street. When I asked the only person in the café, a woman behind the bar, if this was the place the artist Van Gogh had died, she slid a large key along the bar and signaled toward the narrow stairs through a doorway. I climbed the steep steps and unlocked that stifling, windowless, attic room. I opened the small hatch in the ceiling that allowed in the only natural light and breath of fresh air. The artist's own sense of solitude seemed to pervade the cramped space under that café roof.

Later that day I walked the few blocks of the main street, turned off at the Romanesque church Vincent had painted, and walked uphill through the fields of ripe wheat to the village cemetery. Against one stone wall of the cemetery were two similar headstones with the words, "Ici Repose Vincent van Gogh 1853–1890" and "Ici Repose Theodore van Gogh, 1857–1891." Someone had placed a sunflower on each of the graves along with a few stalks of ripe wheat. Ivy bound the two grave-sites together.

I spent the late afternoon on a worn dirt path among the wheatfields musing on the painting of empty shoes I had seen that morning, and the empty paths among the wheatfields where I now stood at sunset. That night, in a rented room on the main street of Auvers, I wrote an essay on my musings that I titled "Empty Shoes on Empty Paths." That is the essay I sent as an answer to Zen Master Kobori-Sohaku who had posed his "koan" years before: "a Van Gogh sunflower and a Mu-ch'i persimmon: are they the same or different?" A month later, back at my university office, I received the essay back again. I had lost track of how much time I had spent on my quest. The attached note told me that Master Kobori had died.

The emptiness of the old shoes in Vincent's Paris painting, a theme he returned to several times, and the solitude of those paths that lose themselves in the field of ripe wheat, bring together for me Vincent's own journey of emptying and the Zen Buddhist notion of the deep meaning of emptiness as a giving up of self-centered desires for a deeper participation in the immediate presence of the life of the things closest to one. Even the koan in zen was intended to self-destruct and so empty itself in the act of bringing illumination.

As I stood on that very path that loses itself in the ripe wheat, it came to me that Vincent's painting of a wheatfield torn by a storm, forcing feeding crows to take flight, should be added to the works of the here and now that come closest for Vincent to a Gethsemane scene devoid of a visible Christ or angel. Recall that in our second chapter we quoted Vincent's words to Theo: "Yes, for me the drama of a storm in nature, the drama of sorrow in life, is the best. A 'paradou' is beautiful, but Gethsemane is more beautiful still" (Letter 381). Vincent had written those lines in September of 1883 after getting soaked by a storm while outdoors painting "crooked, windswept trees." That was early in his life as artist. Now, at the end of his life he painted such a storm twisting the ripe wheat to the earth.

Through the past century critics have described that painting of the wheatfield with stormy skies and crows in flight as a depressing and even frightening scene. In my earlier book, *The Shoes of Van Gogh*, I devote chapter 12 to that painting. I quote such distinguished critics as Meyer Shapiro who described the painting as displaying "disturbing violence" and "pathetic disarray," and H. R. Graetz who viewed the painting's path as a "dead end," and the crows as "sinister and forboding." Even Jan Hulsker calls the work "a doom filled painting with threatening skies and ill-omened crows."[3] In those pages of *The Shoes of Van Gogh* (113–33), I reject such depressing and limiting interpretations. Rather, I describe the painting as a deep and hopeful harvest hymn. But now I see that it is even more than that. It embodies the paradoxes Vincent found in Saint Paul's "sorrowful yet always rejoicing . . . having nothing yet possessing everything," and relates to Zen Buddhism's emptiness and negation that is actually a fullness that is open to and shares in everything.

Vincent's letter of 1883 relating storm, sorrow, and Gethsemane, in fact, finds a breadth and depth in his experience of the storm he just witnessed, an emptiness that opens to the whole of society and its needs. To put his words relating storm and Gethsemane in context, I quote a larger piece of that letter. He writes of that storm:

3. Shapiro, *Vincent van Gogh*, 130; Graetz, *The Symbolic Language*, 278; Hulsker, *The Complete Van Gogh*, 480.

In it I saw an image of how even a person of absurd forms and conventions, or another full of eccentricity and caprice, can become a dramatic figure of special character if he's gripped by true sorrow, moved by a calamity. It made me think for a moment of society today, how as it founders it now often appears like a large, somber silhouette viewed against the light of reform. Yes, for me the drama of a storm in nature, the drama of sorrow in life is best. A "paradou" is beautiful, but Gethsemane is more beautiful still. (Letter 381)

At the end of his life, painting similar storms in the fields of Auvers, painting in fact his *Wheatfield under Stormy Skies with Crows*, Vincent could make clear the paradoxical unity of suffering and joy, sadness and healing he discovered. He wrote Theo and wife Jo:

They're immense stretches of wheatfields under turbulent skies, and I made a point of trying to express sadness, extreme loneliness. You'll see this soon, I hope—for I hope to bring them to you in Paris as soon as possible, since I'd almost believe that these canvases will tell you what I can't say in words, what I consider healthy and fortifying about the countryside. (Letter 898)

This unity of apparent opposites, this enfolding of joy and health within loneliness and sorrow, likewise joined unhappiness and happiness, germination and death in his musings on the wheatfield he painted earlier through his barred window in the Saint Rémy asylum. He interpreted a reaper he saw there as "the image of death, in the sense that humanity might be the wheat he is reaping" (Letter 800). He wrote Theo of the unity of sowing, germination, and bread on the one hand, and death and disappearance on the other:

I feel so strongly that the story of people is like the story of wheat, if one isn't sown in the earth to germinate there, what does it matter, one is milled in order to become bread.
The difference between happiness and unhappiness, both are necessary and useful, and death or passing away... it's so relative—and so is life. (Letter 805)

Through all his moments of ecstasy painting in the fields and orchards, and through all his moments of suffering through illness and loneliness, Vincent had come to accept the paradox of the Bible's "sorrowful yet always rejoicing," not unlike Zen's sense of the unity of life and death, presence and absence. Sowing and reaping, storm and wheat fields, were among the many symbols Vincent seems to have viewed as so natural that one must admit that they are aspects of everyday life at the same moment they are symbols that reach across cultures to offer depth and breadth to the very art of living. In the work of great artists, such as Millet, he wrote Theo, "all reality is also symbolic at the same time" (Letter 533).

It does not seem to me so difficult to understand Vincent shooting himself with a borrowed pistol in a wheatfield in Auvers. He was deeply disturbed that his young sister-in-law and his god-child had been ill. Theo had not only been frantic that their child might die, but felt that his own job at the Montmartre Gallery, their means of support, was threatened. Vincent felt himself to be approaching another health crisis, a further drain on Theo's fragile finances. Might one who painted a Bible open to the Isaiah passage extolling a suffering servant willing to give up his life for others consider sacrificing himself for those he loved? Just four days before he shot himself, Vincent had written the fragment of a letter he was composing for Theo. In it he wrote of his relief that Theo and Jo's child was improving, adding "Since that's going well, which is the main thing, should I go on about things of lesser importance?" He then assured Theo "you have your part in the very production of certain canvases, which even in calamity retain their calm" ("Related Manuscripts," 25). On Sunday, July 27 Vincent shot himself while out painting in an Auvers wheatfield, and he died in his rented attic room in Auvers on July 29, smoking his pipe and sharing with Theo his remembrances of their boyhood and his desire now to die.

That brings me back to the famous Zen koan I placed at the opening of this work:

> A monk asked Master Joshu: "When I bring nothing at all with me, what do you say?"
>
> Master Joshu answered: "Throw it away."

Having renounced creating traditional religious paintings, the very sort of paintings that nourished his own spirituality, Vincent found himself once again in a Gethsemane that asked of him a willingness to dispose of even his struggle as an artist. He had given up the lure of creating religious paintings like those of several masters he admired. He had chosen to paint the things closest to him as the true incarnation of the spiritual. Now he would give up even his art on behalf of the new family of Theo, Jo, and their child.

In his own Gethsemane, Vincent seemed to have come to realize that both his works of art and even his making of art were not to take precedence over the ordinary lives of those who loved and cared for each other, whether peasants and the earth they worked, the new city laborers and their struggles, or the parents who tended a cradle that held the fragile hopes of the future.

The book *Bacon Picasso: The Life of Images* contains these words of Giles Deleuze:

> A canvas is no blank surface. It is already cluttered with clichés, even if one can't see them. The painter's task consists in destroying them . . . the painter has to integrate a catastrophe that becomes the very matrix of the picture.[4]

Dramatic examples of such emptying and destruction might be multiplied, from John Cage creating his "three minute forty-four second" silent piano piece that empties itself of music to allow the sounds of the restless audience to become the music, to Robert Rauschenberg's creation of a new work through his erasure of a valued de Kooning drawing.

Van Gogh's own struggle with the relation of religious traditions and art have been continued and dramatized in our own time by such works as Barnett Newman's *The Stations of the Cross: Lema Sabachthani* and by Mark Rothko's fourteen paintings in black with hints of subdued color in the Rothko Chapel in Houston, Texas. Just as Vincent emptied his olive groves of Christ and the angel, Newman empties the stations of the cross of Christ and related characters in the drama, allowing stripes of black and white on raw canvas to tell, or to withhold, the story. Stories in stained-glass windows often associated with Christian places of worship are refused and replaced by Rothko's fourteen somber paintings without figure and with little beyond shades of black in the Rothko Chapel.

Vincent's life as artist was a giving up of the route of traditional religious art that had meant so much to his own personal spiritual journey, and the key moment in that renunciation was his creation and destruction of the Gethsemane paintings. Those paintings themselves were a chosen scene in the life of "the greatest of artists" who was willing to give up his own life. Vincent imitated that very act, first in giving up his brief experiment in painting the great biblical scenes, and then giving up his very life as artist. Perhaps it was such a sacrifice that has wed Vincent's Gethsemane choice to his body of work and given the whole its depth of meaning. Vincent's life and work might be viewed as a sort of koan that maintains its poignancy for the viewer through a constant emptying of clichés in the "catastrophe that

4. Beldassari, *Bacon Picasso*, 16.

becomes the very matrix of the picture." Perhaps it is only such emptying, beginning with the destruction of the ghost paintings themselves, that in Vincent's life created "symbols for a level of reality that cannot be reached in any other way."[5] That may well be the invitation to empty ourselves in order to risk the journey "to see the universe through the eyes of another."

5. Tillich, *Dynamics of Faith*, 42; Proust, *In Remembrance of Things Past*, 3:762.

Afterword

Our journey of discovery has had more to do with the direction and manner of our exploration than with any attained destination. Responding to the need to reconsider the relation of religion to the arts, I have focused on the incarnation of that struggle in the life of one of the world's most famous artists, Vincent van Gogh. The nature of his serious religious quest and his passionate search for a new art qualify him uniquely as a flesh-and-blood demonstration of the religion and arts struggle of his day and our own.

My inviting you on this journey leaves me with the responsibility for suggesting a few of my own provisional discoveries and directions for further exploration. First, I have been amazed how easily scholars are led to focus on "what exists," as in Van Gogh's paintings and drawings in museums or picture books, to the exclusion of what may have been of primary importance: what was destroyed. Are we so easily tricked into forgetting or omitting key evidence simply because it has been canceled, refused, or otherwise destroyed? Postmodernism's emphasis on erasure and the crucial significance of absence, whether harking back to Freud and the repressed, to Zen philosophy's creative emptiness, to themes in Wittgenstein, Heidegger, Deleuze, or to the experiments of such artists as Raushenberg, Barnett Newman, or Rothko, should both warn and summon us to know what we don't know and to see what can no longer be seen. In the case of Van Gogh and the religion-arts struggle, I believe such knowing of not-knowing and seeing of what can no longer be seen is crucial. Certainly it must be equally significant in the study of other figures in religion and the arts, as well as in self-understanding and a thoughtful critique of culture. So my focus on the "ghost paintings" is quite deliberate and, I believe, critical for a deeper understanding of both Vincent van Gogh and of the relation between religion and art.

Second, but related, is the issue of locating Van Gogh's "religious art." Many have a ready list of his "religious paintings," his three "copies" of works by his admired predecessors, Rembrandt and Delacroix. But do his *Pietà* and *Good Samaritan* after Delacroix and his version of the *Raising of Lazarus* after Rembrandt lead us or mislead us regarding the "religious" in his art? Even if one extends this list to include references to his focus on images from the parables, his many Millet-style sowers and reapers, or even his possible use of color to designate a Christ-presence, have we gotten at the key works crucial to his sense of the meeting of religion and art? Would we do better to view his olive orchards, purposely emptied of Christ and the angel, including his painting of an olive orchard with peasants harvesting olives, in the place we might imagine a Christ? Further, doesn't the artist himself indicate that his choice of the melancholic, suffering Dr. Gachet is his closest attempt at Christ, the wounded healer? Doesn't he call his friend Bernard's attention to the painting of a broken tree and last rose at the asylum garden as the most effective view of Gethsemane? And would we then still be too limited? Is it the cradle, the young child, the sprouting wheat, ripe wheat under a stormy sky, butterflies, revelatory moments on a hillside or in a garden, undergrowth, a clump of grass, that call for our meditative attention? Is "religious art" a way of seeing rather than a what is seen? Have we located Van Gogh's sense of the "natural symbols of the earth?" Perhaps we are led toward interpreting Vincent's art of the here and now as related to the art of the gospel parable. And perhaps it is the "invisible" process of his art, its creation and destruction that is closest to the heart of his quest.

Third, have we focused too often on a one-dimensional religious Van Gogh, a Van Gogh who is either for or against traditional religion at this or that time in his life? Might we better think of a complex artist-religious seeker who admits to certain traditional religious needs for comfort, to certain images of Christ he wants on his wall, but an artist whose eyes are on an inaccessible horizon in both religion and art that ventures beyond the traditional? We have suggested that there is the Van Gogh nourished by some works of traditional religious art, which feed his own hidden spirituality, and there is another Van Gogh who seeks a hidden art of the future striving to abandon the clichés of the past in his own creative explorations. Certainly for me our focus on "ghost paintings" has led to a far deeper and broader understanding of both the simplicity and the complexity of Van Gogh's life and work.

The eyes with which we see Van Gogh are also a critical issue. As I write, I admit that my recent reading in Gilles Deleuze, Masao Abe and the Kyoto School, and several other scholars at the edge of a new vision of art, meaning, and creativity have caused me to see elements in religion and the arts that I had not seriously considered before. Here I might, for example, note Gilles Deleuze's views of the meaning of inside and outside, enfolding and unfolding, views found in his work *The Fold: Leibniz and the Baroque*. The image of "the fold" seems especially useful to me as I consider the complexity of Van Gogh's search within religion and art for some possibility of a unifying harmony enfolded at the heart of tensions and struggle.

Finally, I will simply note that Van Gogh's fear of success in art, his preference for the poor and dispossessed, the forgotten and abandoned, strike me as essential in understanding his life and work and its relevance for us. Related to these preferences is his personal discovery that the paradoxical enfolding of joy within suffering, a paradox he finds in Paul's letters, became his provisional guide in life: "as sorrowful, yet always rejoicing; as poor, yet making many rich; as having nothing, and yet possessing everything" (2 Corinthians 6:10). In this sense of Pauline paradox, Van Gogh seems to have found the positive folded within the negative, joy as located not on its own or as prior, but as requiring the journey through sorrow, suffering, and negation. How poignant that the artist's giving up his Gethsemane paintings recapitulates the very meaning of Gethsemane in the gospels. Sacrificing personal preference for a deeper and broader mission requiring destruction is a process both journeys have in common. Freedom calls the spiritual guide and the artist to an empty path through negation toward the affirmation of an undetermined future. Van Gogh's choice of Gethsemane and its agonizing decision to accept a broader and deeper truth is therefore a crucial element in his understanding of the Bible and art. This focus on lonely choice with its burden of rejection and suffering relativizes even the artist's devotion to art. Van Gogh offers us the insight that it is not at the cross, whose reality is determined by those in authority, but rather at Gethsemane, where personal decision must remain creatively alert, that a new understanding of the gospel story and the future of both religion and art are to be realized.

Select Bibliography

Apostolos-Cappadona, Diane, editor. *Art, Creativity, and the Sacred*. New York: Crossroad, 1986.

―――. *Dictionary of Christian Art*. New York:Continuum, 1994.

Balzac, Honoré. *César Birotteau*. Translated by Frances Frenaye. New York: Juniper, 1955.

Beldassari, Anne. *Bacon Picasso: The Life of Images*. New York: Rizzoli International, 2005.

Bogue, Ronald. *Deleuze on Music, Painting, and Other Arts*. New York, Routledge, 2003.

Brooks, David. *Vincent van Gogh: The Complete Works*. CD-ROM Database. Sharon, MA: Barewalls, 2002.

Brown, Raymond. *The Death of the Messiah: From Gethsemane to the Grave: A Commentary on the Passion Narratives*. New York: Doubleday, 1994.

Collins, Adela Yarbro. *Gospel of Mark: A Commentary*. Hermeneia. Minneapolis: Fortress, 2007.

Davidson, Charles. *Bone Dead, and Rising: Vincent van Gogh and the Self Before God*. Eugene, OR: Cascade, 2012.

Deleuze, Giles. *The Fold: Leibniz and the Baroque*. Translated by Tom Conley. Minneapolis: University of Minnesota Press, 1993.

Dixon, John Wesley. *Art and the Theological Imagination*. New York: Seabury, 1978.

Edwards, Cliff. *Mystery of the Night Café: Hidden Key to the Spirituality of Vincent van Gogh*. Excelsior Editions. Albany, NY: State University of New York, 2009.

―――. *The Shoes of Van Gogh: A Spiritual and Artistic Journey to the Ordinary*. New York: Crossroad, 2004.

―――. *Van Gogh and God: A Creative Spiritual Quest*: Chicago: Loyola University Press, 1989.

Erickson, Kathleen Powers. *At Eternity's Gate: The Spiritual Vision of Vincent van Gogh*. Grand Rapids: Eerdmans, 1998.

Graetz, H. R. *The Symbolic Language of Vincent Van Gogh*. New York: McGraw-Hill, 1963.

Halewood, William. *Six Subjects of Reformation Art: A Preface to Rembrandt*. Toronto: University of Toronto Press, 1982.

Harries, Karsten. *Art Matters: A Critical Commentary on Heidegger's "The Origin of the Work of Art."* Contributions to Phenomenology 57. Dordrecht: Springer, 2009.

Harrison, Robert. *Van Gogh's Letters: Unabridged and Annotated*. No pages. Online: http://www.webexhibits.org/vangogh/.

Heidegger, Martin. "The Origin of the Work of Art." In *Basic Writings from* Being and Time *to the Task of Thinking*, edited by David Krell, 163–83. New York: Harper and Row, 1977.

Homburg, Cornelia. *The Copy Turns Original: Vincent van Gogh and a New Approach to Traditional Art Practice*. Philadelphia: Benjamins, 1996.

———. *The Treasures of Vincent Van Gogh*. New York: Metro, 2007.

Hulsker, Jan. *The Complete Van Gogh*. New York: Abrams, 1980.

———. *The New Complete Van Gogh*. Amsterdam: Meulenhoff, 1996.

———. *Vincent and Theo Van Gogh: A Dual Biography*. Edited by James Miller. Ann Arbor, MI: Fuller, 1990.

Jansen, Leo, et al. *Vincent van Gogh: The Letters*. In *The Museum Letters Project*, 6 volumes. Amsterdam: Van Gogh Museum and Huygens Institute, 2009. Online: http://www. Vangoghletters.org/vg/.

Kodera, Tsukasa, editor. *The Mythology of Vincent Van Gogh*. Amsterdam: Benjamins, 1993.

Loti, Pierre. *Madame Chrysanthème*. London: Routledge, n.d.

MacGregor, Neil. *Seeing Salvation: Images of Christ in Art*. New Haven, CT: Yale University Press, 2000.

Masao, Abe. "Man and Nature in Christianity and Buddhism." In *The Buddha Eye: An Anthology of the Kyoto School,* edited by Frederick Franck, 148–56. New York: Crossroad, 1982.

Masheck, Joseph, editor. *Van Gogh 100*. Westport, CT: Greenwood, 1996.

Pickvance, Ronald. *Van Gogh in Arles*. New York: Abrams, 1984.

———. *Van Gogh in Saint-Rémy and Auvers*. New York: Abrams, 1986.

Proust, Marcel. *A la recherche du temps perdu*. 3 volumes. Paris: Gallimard, 1988.

Renan, Ernest. *La Vie de Jésus*. Paris: Michel Levy, 1863.

Rilke, Rainer Maria. *Letters on Cézanne*. New York: Farrar, Straus, and Giroux, 2002.

Shapiro, Meyer. *Vincent Van Gogh*. Garden City, New York: Doubleday, 1980.

Sheon, Aaron. *Monticelli: His Contemporaries, His Influence*. Pittsburg: Museum of Art, Carnegie Institute, 1978.

Silverman, Deborah. *Van Gogh and Gauguin: The Search for Sacred Art*. New York: Farrar, Straus, and Giroux, 2000.

Steiner, George. *My Unwritten Books*. London: Weidenfeld and Nicolson, 2008.

Stevens, Mary Ann, editor. *Emile Bernard: A Pioneer of Modern Art*. Amsterdam: Van Gogh Museum, n.d.

Stolwijk, Chris, and Thomson, Richard, editors. *Theo Van Gogh: Art Dealer, Collector and Brother of Vincent*. Amsterdam: Van Gogh Museum, n.d.

Sund, Judy. *True to Temperament: van Gogh and French Naturalist Literature*. New York: Cambridge University Press, 1992.

———. *Van Gogh*. London: Phaidon, 2002.

Thomson, Iain. *Heidegger, Art, and Postmodernity*. Cambridge: Cambridge University Press, 2011.

Tillich, Paul. *Dynamics of Faith*. New York: Harper and Row, 1957.

Tralbaut, Marc. *Vincent Van Gogh*. Lausanne: Edita Lausanne, 1969.

Van Gogh, Theo, and Jo Bonger. *Brief Happiness: The Correspondence of Theo van Gogh and Jo Bonger*. Edited by Leo Jansen and Jan Robert. Amsterdam: Van Gogh Museum, 1999.

Van Gogh, Vincent. *The Complete Letters of Vincent van Gogh*. Edited by Johanna van Gogh-Bonger. 3 volumes. Boston: Little Brown, 1978.

Whitford, Frank. *Japanese Prints and Western Painters*. London: Studio Vista, 1977.

Wichman, Siegfried. *Japonisme*. New York: Park Lane, 1985.

Zemel, Carol. *The Formation of a Legend: Van Gogh Criticism, 1890–1920*. Ann Arbor: UMI Research Press, 1980.

———. *Van Gogh's Progress: Utopia, Modernity, and Late-Nineteenth-Century Art*. Berkeley, CA: University of California Press, 1997.

Zola, Emile. *The Sin of Father Mouret*. Translated by Sandy Petrey. Englewood Cliffs, NJ: Prentice-Hall, 1969.

FIGURE 1

CHRIST CONSOLATEUR

Engraving of Ary Scheffer's **Christus Consolator**

Amsterdam Historisch Museum, on loan to the Van Gogh Museum

Letter from Vincent to brother Theo, January 21, 1877: "The two prints, 'Christus Consolator' and 'Remunerator,' which you gave me are hanging in my little room—I saw the pictures at the museum as well as Scheffer's 'Christ in Gethsemane,' which in unforgettable." (Letter 101)

Ary Scheffer's **Christ in Gethsemane** can be seen on the internet at vangoghletters.org, Letter 101, artwork

FIGURE 2

Vincent van Gogh, oil painting, **Still Life with Open Bible and Zola Novel**, 1885 Nuenen, Van Gogh Museum

Letter 537, October 28, 1885: "I'm enclosing . . . a Bible they gave me for you at home, of which I made a still life."

The Bible is open to a "Suffering Servant Song" in Isaiah, chapter fifty-three, and the Zola novel *is La Joie de Vivre*

FIGURE 3

Vincent Van Gogh oil painting, **Pair of Old Shoes**, Paris, summer to autumn 1886, Van Gogh Museum

See Chapter 14 of this work, "Empty Shoes on Empty Paths."

FIGURE 4

Vincent van Gogh drawing, **The Rock of Montmajour with Trees**, 1888, Arles, Van Gogh Museum

Letter 636, Vincent to Theo, July 5, 1888: "Yesterday at sunset, I was on a stony heath where very small twisted oaks grow, in the background a ruin on the hill . . .the sun was pouring its very yellow rays over the bushes and the ground, absolutely a shower of gold."

FIGURE 5

Lithograph by Nanteuil after Delacroix's **Pietà**, spoiled in oil in Vincent van Gogh's asylum room in September, 1889. Vincent van Gogh wrote Theo on September 10, 1889: "Thus this time during my illness a misfortune happened to me—that lithograph of Delacroix, the **Pietà**, with other sheets had fallen into some oil and paint and got spoiled . . . I occupied myself painting it, and you'll see it one day.

FIGURE 6

Vincent van Gogh's oil painting, **Pietà**, after the spoiled lithograph by Nanteuil of Delacroix's **Pietà**, Van Gogh Museum

See Letter 801, September 10, 1889

FIGURE 7

Paul Gauguin's Letter to Vincent van Gogh, Letter 817, November, 1889, with Gauguin's sketch of the Gauguin painting, **Christ in the Garden of Olives**, Van Gogh Museum

Gauguin writes: "It's a Christ in the Garden of Olives . . . As this canvas isn't destined to be understood I'm keeping it for a long time."

FIGURE 8

Vincent Van Gogh oil painting, **Olive Orchard**, November 1889, Van Gogh Museum

Vincent's letter 820 to Theo, November 19, 1889: "If I remain here I wouldn't try to paint a Christ in the Garden of Olives, but in fact the olive picking as it's still seen today . . . "

FIGURE 9

Rembrandt's etching **Raising of Lazarus**, Van Gogh Museum collection

FIGURE 10

Van Gogh sketch of a detail from Rembrandt's **Raising of Lazarus**, in Letter 866 to Theo, May 2, 1890

Vincent wrote Theo, on page one of letter 866: "The etchings you sent me are really beautiful. Opposite this I've scribbled a croquis after a painting I've done of three figures which are in the background of the Lazarus etching. The dead man and his two sisters."

FIGURE 11

Vincent Van Gogh etching, **Portrait of Dr. Gachet with Pipe**, G1664, etching, collection of the Anderson Gallery, Virginia Commonwealth University

This etching was made at Dr. Gachet's home in Auvers by Vincent after he had painted Dr. Gachet's portrait in oils. Of his oil painting of Dr. Gachet seated at a table with a foxglove plant, Vincent wrote Gauguin in a letter never mailed (RM 23): "Now I have a portrait of Dr. Gachet with the deeply sad expression of our time. If you like something like you were saying of your Christ in the Garden of Olives, not destined to be understood . . ." The color portrait of Dr. Gachet can be seen on the internet at vangoghletters.org, RM 23 (related manuscripts 23), artworks.

Index of Paintings and Prints of Christ in Gethsemane Mentioned in the Van Gogh Correspondence

(Going to www.vangoghletters.org/vh/letters.html and scrolling to the Letter number, and clicking "artworks" will provide these images)

1. Letter 034 Vincent to Theo, May 31, 1875
Jean Baptiste Camille Corot: **Christ on the Mount of Olives**

2. Letter 055 Vincent to Theo, October 11, 1875
Ernest Hebert : **Christ on the Mount of Olives (Kiss of Judas)**

3. Letter 084 Vincent to Theo, June 17, 1876
Paul Delaroche: **Christ on the Mount of Olives**

4. Letter 101 Vincent to Theo, January 21, 1877
Ary Sheffer: **Christ in Gethsemane**

5. Letter 148 Vincent to Theo, November 1, 1878
Carlo Dolci: **Christ in Gethsemane**
Rembrandt van Rijn: **Christ In Gethsemane**

6. Letter 817 Paul Gauguin to Vincent, Nov. 10-13, 1889
Paul Gauguin: **Christ in the Garden of Olives**

7. Letter 819 Theo to Vincent, November 16, 1889
Emile Bernard: **Christ in the Garden of Olives**

Index of Books and Authors